Out of the Closet

By Autumn Bailey

Library of Congress Control Number: 2008907410

ISBN: 978-0-615-19746-3

First Printing   November, 2008

Printed in the U.S.A. by
Morris Publishing
3212 East Highway 30
Kearney, NE 68847
1-800-650-7888

DEDICATION

To my Deliverer, Jesus Christ, the Righteous . . . words are too shallow . . . You've captured my heart.

To every person who has experienced the war and torment of perversion, specifically homosexuality . . . the love, peace, and freedom that you seek can be found only in Jesus Christ.

TABLE OF CONTENTS

FOREWORD

Saint Paul said, "We are living epistles seen and read of all men . . ." We are the gospel that men see today. Like Paul's message, our gospel is the testimony of our experience as Christians since Jesus Christ became our Savior.

Never have I read from any Christian a testimony more candid than this story of *Out of the Closet.*

It is easy to write "our gospel" of how we built the biggest church in America. It is encouraging to read the gospels of those who had miracles of healing and salvation. But I thank God for this young woman who stands boldly and nakedly in the eyes of the world to say courageously, "Now unto Him who is able to do exceeding abundantly above all that most Christians will testify to, it is to Him I bring the glory of my testimony. The glory of my gospel."

Thank God for this one who is not ashamed of the gospel of her salvation.

Hazel Dawson
Pastor, The F.O.L.D. Church

ACKNOWLEDGMENTS

To Pastor Hazel Dawson….thank you for all of your words of wisdom, guidance, time, support, and endless efforts in assisting me, not only in my Christian walk, but with this book. Most of all, thank you for the best advice I have ever received: "You need to put your face to the wall, pray, and rebuke the devil!"

To Pastor James Dawson . . . a man of God who taught me to trust. Thank you for listening, understanding, and helping me to understand myself. Most of all, thank you for teaching me the importance of prayer by exemplifying it in your life. Many thanks for sharing your photography skills for the cover of this book.

To the best mom in the whole wide world . . . the only one I love more is Jesus.

To my Dad, Lew...thank you for raising me as your own. Most of all, thank you for coming back for me. I love you.

To Sharon "Susie" Hill…my mentor, my sister, my friend. Thank you for taking me under your wing.

To Evelyn Irving-Jackson…thank you so much for all of your hard work, dedication and patience in preparing this manuscript for publication.

PROLOGUE

The consequences of living as a lesbian resulted in a heavy burden. I desperately sought deliverance. I didn't realize at the time that I was entrapped by a spirit and that the burden was caused by bondage. I was held captive by a spirit that brought with it oppression, loneliness, guilt, and shame. I wanted to be delivered. I knew I was being held a prisoner but did not know my jailor. I only knew that I was not free. That is the nature of bondage. It has you entwined like a ball of yarn that cannot be untangled.

The nature of bondage is the same, whether it is to drugs, alcohol, gambling, or pornography. Bondage leaves you feeling trapped, which causes you to be unhappy, miserable, alone, and lonely. I was in bondage to homosexuality. But today, by the power and process of the Holy Ghost, I am delivered.

THE VISION

It all began on a round island with white sand and crystal blue waters in the middle. There is absolutely no sign of life around. It is just Jesus and me on the island. Jesus walks in front of me, and I follow about twenty feet behind. I am fully clothed in pants, shirts, a jacket, boots, mittens, earmuffs, and undergarments. My clothes are very dirty. I walk very slowly, dragging myself to keep up with Jesus. My eyes are focused on the white sands directly below me. My body is completely hunched over. I stumble and even fall countless times. Every time that I stumble, Jesus stops, turns around, and looks at me without speaking a word. Each time that I stumble, I slowly get myself together and continue to follow Jesus in circles around the island.

As I continue to stumble, I realize that my dirty clothes have been weighing me down. The heaviness of the clothes causes me to stumble and sometimes fall. If I could just remove some of the clothes, I would be able to follow Jesus. The clothes have been holding me back.

In this vision each piece of clothing represents a negative behavior, a bad habit, an issue from my past, or one of my insecurities. First I take off the earmuffs and continue to walk. Soon I realize that I need to remove something else. Each time that I shed a piece of clothing, my body straightens a little more. My eyes no longer focus on the sand beneath me. I can look up enough to see the feet of Jesus walking ahead of me. Even though I am no longer stumbling, I can still feel Jesus turning around and making sure that I am still behind Him. As I stay determined to follow the Lord, more and more clothes begin to come off me. I no longer have to pull them off, but they begin to fall off on their own.

Now I am naked, walking completely upright, with my eyes fixed on Jesus. Only this time Jesus turns his body completely around, smiles, and asks me, "Are you ready?' and I say, "Yes, Lord." He then motions for me to come. I slowly walk toward Him. I bow down to His feet and thank Him for His strength, His patience, and His everlasting, unconditional love. He then motions for me to rise to my feet. Jesus and I then walk side by side. We are no longer walking in circles around the island but walk straight toward the light of the sun.

This is my vision. This is where I long to be. Through the weightiness, the stumbling, the falling, Jesus has always been there, waiting for me and watching over me. I used to walk in darkness, clothed in filthy garments with my head and my eyes pointed toward the sand. But these clothes have fallen off me, and I can now see the feet of the Lord Jesus Christ. I am determined to walk forward, without falling or turning back to pick up those clothes. I want to be naked, standing upright, looking into the eyes of my Savior, my Lord, and my forever friend Jesus Christ.

INTRODUCTION

Positioned in one place, transitioning to the next place. Stumbling, walking, running. Whatever it takes to move beyond all that has tried to weigh you down. A by-any-means-necessary mentality. An honest look into your heart. A place where no masks are applied. You've got me open, Lord.

You can either be processed in or be processed out. You do not just float from one place to the other. You move through the process to get to where God is calling you. The process is painful, rough, and uneasy. The process is confusing, loud, and heavy at times. The process breaks you down but only to build you back up. The process rocks your world. It shakes you to the very core of your being. It uproots your foundation and lays a new one. You will be poured out, to be poured into, in order to be poured out for others.

Deliverance is a process—a necessary process that God uses to set you free. He does it not only for your personal benefit but so that you can be used in the lives of others who need to be processed. Whatever your issues are, the Lord wants to take you through the process to deliver you so that you can be broken bread for others.

People everywhere need to be processed. People of different races, cultures, and ages. The necessity of the process does not discriminate. Everyone has gone through battles that have left them bleeding on the inside. Everyone has wounds that need to be cleansed, stitched, and completely healed. We have unresolved issues in our lives that have followed us through the years. Yes, we may be saved already, and yes, we may love Jesus already, but we need deliverance.

Introduction

When we come to the altar, confess Jesus Christ as Lord, and ask Him to forgive us for our sins, we are saved. Those issues from our past—our shortcomings, negative behaviors, and bad habits—follow us out the door of the church, however. We leave church that day saved, but we need to go through the process to be delivered.

The Lord desires to make His people whole. He has a work for the Body of Christ to accomplish. Our effectiveness in the kingdom of God is a direct result of our willingness to allow the Lord to take us through the process of deliverance.

The purpose of this book is not to shock you with my sin or seek glory for myself. The only part of my testimony worth bragging about is that Jesus Christ, the Son of the Living God, had mercy on me. I gain no prestige from man for the writing of this book. As a matter of fact, I am not proud of the issues that I reveal in these pages. Held in bondage by the shame that came with my sin, I could not share my testimony openly. The shame alone was debilitating. But today I can show you my scars, hoping that someone will come to know Jesus Christ not only as Savior, but as Deliverer.

As you read through the pages of this book, I pray that you will allow the Lord to begin to process the pages of your life. I pray that you would begin to see your relationship with Christ in a whole new dimension. The Lord has plans for your life. Although the process can be painful, it is necessary for your spiritual growth, and it is vital to the Body of Christ. It doesn't matter what issues you may be struggling with. Whether you know Jesus as your Lord and Savior or you don't, you have been divinely appointed to hold this book in your hands right now. Let's pray…

Father, in the name of Jesus, I thank You for drawing me to read this book. My earnest prayer is that as I read, You would begin to reveal to me the hidden recesses of my heart. Shine Your divine light on every area of my life. Lord, I want to be delivered from everything that holds me in bondage. I want to be delivered from every issue from my past. I want to be delivered from issues that have held me captive for so many years. Father, open my heart and my mind to receive from You. I rebuke the enemy of my soul who would try to condemn me. I rebuke the spirit of shame from my life. Lord, I am ready to deal with my issues. I am ready for You to have Your way in my life. You alone are God, and I trust You with my life. Have Your way, Lord. In Jesus' name, amen.

1. BORN IN SIN

I was born on August 21, 1974 in Oceanside, California. My father and mother never married. Shortly after my first birthday my parents separated. By the time I was three, my mother met my stepfather, who has been a father to me throughout my life. My stepfather, an asbestos worker, and my mother, a topless dancer, both used drugs heavily; marijuana, crystal methamphetamine, uppers, downers, hallucinogens, pharmaceuticals, alcohol, nicotine, and the most destructive heroin and cocaine.

For the first nineteen years of my life, drugs ruled our home. My mother was addicted to heroin, cocaine, and alcohol. My stepfather, who was addicted to crystal meth, smoked marijuana daily. My mother was either asleep all day, nodding off from the heroin; cleaning house vigorously while on cocaine; intoxicated while dancing at a topless bar; or out stealing to support her drug habit. My stepfather worked during the day and came home either in a rage or as the sweetest man on earth due to the mood swings that are typical with crystal use.

I didn't know that my parents' lifestyle was abnormal until I was old enough to spend time at friends' homes. I soon realized that my life was not the way that it was supposed to be. When friends wanted to come to my house, I always went in first to check on my parents' condition. Many times I made excuses as to why I didn't allow my friends in the house. I realized that the activities in my house were not happening at my friends' homes. As a result, I started worrying about my mom and stepfather at an early age.

A lady who lived down the street had given me some smooth rocks. She called them "worry rocks" and told me to rub them with my thumb when I worried. I did sometimes. I remember being so worried about my mother that I opened the bedroom door to look at her while she slept to make sure that she was still breathing.

My mother has always been the closest person to my heart, even in her addiction. Although we didn't spend much of what most people would call "quality time" together, there was no one in the entire world that I loved more than my mother. Throughout the years of her drug use, I wanted nothing more than to be with her. During times of separation I felt so incomplete. I felt as if our hearts were knitted together as one. Her departure ripped my heart in half.

MY EARLY YEARS

When I was six years of age, I had a babysitter who lived down the street from us. She often cared for me on weekends while my mom and stepfather visited the club. She had an uncle, an older man, who lived in the house. He watched me when my babysitter wasn't around. He sometimes fondled me while I lay on the couch. I never tried to stop him. For years I wondered what was wrong with me because I didn't try to fight him off. Why didn't I try to stop him? I never ran away. I just lay there and allowed him to touch me as we watched TV in the living room.

One morning, while I was using the bathroom, he let himself in unannounced. He was not fully clothed. He stood there staring at me, with his pants undone, fully exposed. I did not understand why he did that. Frightened and stunned, I remember walking out of the bathroom in confusion. When I went home later, I wanted to tell my mom what had happened, but I was scared. I finally told my mom that the man had touched me before. When she asked me what had happened, I saw the concern in my mother's eyes. I've always hated to see my mother upset or cry. I believe that's why I retracted my story. I lied and told her that I had made up the story. My mother believed me when I said that I had lied about the whole thing. This experience, coupled with a few other sexually related occurrences with males who were much older than I, deeply impacted me and how I related to men. I began touching myself at an early age. My mother caught me with a neighbor boy and a pornographic magazine in our backyard when I was only six. She discovered us both with our pants pulled down to our ankles, getting ready to try to imitate what we saw in the magazine.

My first sexual experiences, which included heavy kissing and touching, occurred when I was in elementary school. I always was faster than my other friends when I was young. I also played a game with my female friend, which we called "BFGF"—short for boyfriend girlfriend. When we played this game, I was always the boy. Although we never did anything sexually, I liked the feeling that I had when we played the game, and I enjoyed playing the part of the boyfriend.

I got involved with organized softball at age five. My stepfather even coached most of my teams until I got into high school, despite the fact that he—and my mother—continued using drugs. I thank God for sports because through them I learned many life skills, such as discipline, teamwork, obedience, and how to stay focused. At the high school level, I had to maintain my grades to be eligible to play, so that motivated me in the classroom. I played basketball, softball, and volleyball in high school. Basketball and softball followed me to the collegiate level. I had some coaches who really cared about me, watched over me, and gave me direction.

LOSING MOM TO DRUGS

When I was twelve, my mother was sent to jail for close to a year. This happened when my stepfather was out of town working. I was home alone for a few days, not knowing my mother's whereabouts. The family across the street often took care of me in times of crisis. This time, however, I invited some friends over and just hung out at the house. Discovering that I had been home without an adult, this same family had my stepfather contacted. He came home temporarily to get me situated. I was sent to live with a relative for a while. From there I was sent to live with a best friend and her family for about six months.

Finally out of jail, my mother went straight back to heroin and cocaine. By the time I got into high school, I was hanging out with kids who were older. I also started drinking heavily and experimenting with marijuana. All my friends in high school thought my mom was the coolest. She allowed me to cut classes with my friends. Once she even drove us to our destination during school hours. I never had a whole lot of structure, but I did have a curfew, and my stepfather stayed on me about my grades. If I wanted to stay out later, I just got permission to stay the night at friends' homes that didn't necessarily have to be home at a certain hour. I started going to clubs in Tijuana, with my mom's permission, when I was fourteen years old. My parents knew that I drank, and it was never an issue.

I also continued to experiment sexually with young men. Some were my age, but others were older. The girls whom I hung out with at the time were older, and so were these guys. I wouldn't allow these young men to have full intercourse with me. I had a distrust for males that was underlined with fear. I was scared to allow it to happen. This was my way of staying in control of the situation.

By the time I was in tenth grade, my mother was in jail again. This time the court ordered her to complete a residential program called New Entra Casa. Here my mother was introduced to the Lord Jesus Christ. I met my mom at church sometimes. I really liked to go. Every time I went, the Lord ministered to me, and I started to cry. My mother lived in this program for three months. Some really good changes happened in her life while in this program. She didn't stay clean for very long after graduating from this program, however.

TRYING TO COPE

In the meantime, I continued to drink heavily and hang out with my older friends at house parties, hotel parties, and clubs in Tijuana. By this time, my drinking habit had become pretty serious. A friend's mother began to get a little worried. I often came to her home drunk. I remember one stage where I had a bad couple of days in a row. One day I threw up at her house from drinking too much. The next day the police pulled over two friends and me because I had an open container in the car. Our driver was of age. But my friend and I were both fifteen.

She was picked up by her relative. The police couldn't contact my stepfather, and my mom was in the program. The police wanted to take me to juvenile hall, but I told them that I had someone who was like a mother. They released me to the custody of my friend's mom. At this point, my friend's mother thought that maybe I needed to be checked into a program for my continued problems with alcohol. This never happened, and I continued to drink away the pain as often as I could. All the while I was playing organized sports and keeping my grades at an average level.

From the perspective of the average onlooker, my life looked great. I was a really good athlete, popular in school, and had a good sense of humor. But on the inside, I struggled with anxiety, fear, anger, confusion, and darkness. I mastered the art of living behind a slew of defense mechanisms and masks. Only a select few knew what was going on in my home. I clung to those people like my life depended on them.

FEELING ABANDONED

In the middle of my junior year my mother, who had completely relapsed, stunned me with some news. "Autumn, your friend's family will take care of you for a while. Your stepfather is going to move to Idaho to live with his sister, and I'm going to live with a friend of mine."

What really happened?

My stepfather was strung out on cocaine, and my mom was strung out on heroin. After losing his job, my stepfather could no longer pay for the house. He was moving away to live with his sister in Idaho to get clean and sober. My mom ended up living in her car. So here I was, feeling abandoned.

One night, soon before my own move, I came home completely drunk. I threw myself on the grass of the front yard and had a fit. "I don't want to move!" I screamed. Sobbing almost uncontrollably, I lay in the dew-dampened grass. I was scared and didn't know what was going to happen as a result of being separated from both parents at the same time. My stepfather had always been there for me. He took care of me in my mom's addiction, even while struggling with his own. He cared for me as if I was his own. Now he was going to another state, and I didn't know how to handle it. Sandy, my neighbor across the street, heard the commotion, saw me having a tantrum in the front yard, and called my house.

"Hello, I don't know what's going on, but Autumn is lying in your front lawn, yelling and crying. You should probably go out and get her."

The porch door opened up. I turned my head and saw my stepfather's large, muscular silhouette about ten feet away from me.

"Come inside, Autumn," he said in a stern yet concerned voice.

I struggled to my feet, wiped the tears from my eyes, and slowly made my way into the house.

"I don't want to move!" I cried to my mom and Lew. "I want to be with you!"

"It's going to be all right, Autumn," my mom reassured me. "You will only be living with them for a couple of months."

A couple months turned into a year and a half.

AN ANGRY YOUNG WOMAN

After I moved into my friend's home, my mother was sent to jail. After a short stay in the local women's facility, she was transferred to a women's prison in Northern California. I never felt so alone in my life. My mother always meant the world to me, and I could not stand to be separated from her. It scared me to think that she was in prison with hard core criminals. I was scared for her safety.

Before the authorities transferred her to prison, I visited my mother at Las Colinas women's jail. We sat on opposite sides of the glass, talking on the phone. I noticed that the lady in the seat next to her said something to my mom. My mom said something back. I immediately perceived this exchange of words as an attack on my mother.

Bolting to my feet, I knocked my chair over. Gripping the phone and glaring at that woman, I screamed at her through the glass, "I'll kill you if you touch my mom! I'll kill you!" I yelled hysterically as I peered through the thick glass window. The guard came in to the room, yelled, "Times up," and escorted my mom back to her cell.

I left in tears, frightened for my mother's life. I cried on the way home as I replayed in my head what had just happened. Later I discovered that the lady had not threatened my mother at all. I had totally jumped the gun. This shows the instability of my emotions throughout this time in my life.

Another incident inflamed me with rage. A guy came up to me at a party and asked, "Want to dance?" I accepted. Soon after, a girl came over to the two of us. She looked upset and spoke to the guy in a threatening tone of voice. She then turned, looked at me, and said to him, "If you want to dance with this #$&!, then go ahead!" She turned and walked away. Shocked by what she said, I immediately followed her to the door and began antagonizing her.

"What did you call me? What did you call me?" I repeated.

The girl kept walking. I started to turn around and said, "Yeah, that's what I thought." As soon as I turned my head to walk the other way, a fist came flying through the air and caught me in the lower jaw. I later found out that I turned around, gave her a cold hard stare, smiled, and started throwing blows. I blacked out because of the violent anger inside me. I continued to punch the girl in the face. It wasn't until I was pulled off her that I came out of the blackout. No one who was close to me expected this behavior from me. But I had so much seething just below the surface that, if provoked, my anger boiled over.

By my senior year, Child Protective Services had found out about my situation and began to seek me out. They showed up at my school and got me out of class to speak with them in the office. I saw them as the enemy. They just wanted to take me away and steal me from my mother. They asked me many questions, but I never gave them too much information.

Because my friend's family did not have legal guardianship of me, CPS wanted to place me elsewhere. Devastated by another change, I threatened to run. Anxiety took over. My friend's family agreed to get a foster care license and continued to host me in their home. I spent the remainder of my senior year in their home.

Just before graduating from high school, I told my stepfather that I wanted to be with him. That was all it took. He began making arrangements. Right after graduation, he and I moved into a house. My mom got out of prison shortly after that, and she joined us.

CONFRONTING MOM

Prison did not help my mother's addiction. She got out and continued to use. She tried to be sneakier about it, but I found out. One day she had asked to use my jeep. Later, when I got into my jeep, I found a needle in a bag. I remember being so upset. Her addiction bothered me, but I couldn't believe she had the audacity to use my car to handle her business. I took the needle and went to my mother. I held it up and dropped it in front of her.

"You left this in my car," I told her. Then I stormed up to my room.

I loathed my mother's addiction. I tried to numb the pain with alcohol and by this time smoked marijuana on a regular basis. My stepfather wasn't doing crystal anymore, but he continued to smoke marijuana.

A friend of mine was heavily into dealing and became his connection. I often picked up my stepfather's supply for him. He shared with me, or I got my own. I smoked to relax. I smoked socially. I smoked on campus and went to classes high. I still had to face all of my problems when I came down from the high. Nothing changed.

When I was nineteen, my college basketball coach convinced me to talk to my mom about how her drug addiction was affecting my life. I was having a difficult time with life and had times where I felt emotionally unstable. Sometimes I just cried for no apparent reason. Once right in the middle of basketball practice, I ran off the court, went into the bathroom, and just cried. I often confided in my coach and told her what was going on in my home.

"Coach, I'm scared that I am going to go home one day and find my mom dead."

"Autumn," my coach said, "you have to talk to her. You have to tell her how her addiction is affecting your life."

"I can't. We never talk about it. It's like that elephant sitting in the middle of the living room that everyone tries to pretend isn't there."

"She needs to know," she said.

I knew that my coach was right. I couldn't go on like this anymore. I felt like I was losing it. Something needed to happen in my mother's life, or I couldn't stay in the house anymore.

I decided to follow through with my coach's advice. I came home from basketball practice and began to let it out. I told my mother the cold, hard truth about how her addiction was affecting my life. It was an emotional conversation filled with many tears. All my mother could do was sit there, listen, cry, and apologize. My mother received the truth of that conversation and five days later checked herself into the hospital. While in the hospital, my mother stuck it out through the wrenching pains of withdrawal. She cried out to the Lord in that hospital, and Jesus heard her cry.

My mom has been saved and drug free for thirteen years now. She is now a head counselor at New Entra Casa, the residential program for women ex-offenders that she graduated from when I was in the tenth grade. She is also the chief financial officer at our church. Our relationship has been completely healed and restored. My stepfather no longer uses crystal or marijuana. It is an absolute miracle! To God be the glory

2. UNLEASHING THE DEMON

Up to this point in my life, I had many close friends both male and female. I stayed out late and often stayed at friends' homes. While doing this, I played sports and tried to keep up my grades. I had a few female friends with whom I was exceptionally close. These friends temporarily filled the void in my life for love, care, concern, safety, and acceptance. The response that I would receive from these few always felt so good and made me feel safe. They made me feel loved and needed.

Going into my senior year of high school, I became very close with one of these female friends. I shared my deepest feelings with her. I felt safe, knowing I could show my emotions in her presence. She was always there to comfort me and to help me in any way that she could. She showed me so much care, concern, and love. We were always together. As she continued to give love, I continued to receive it. In fact, I began to thrive off it.

THE LINE DISAPPEARS

The love later began to turn into lust. Confused, I didn't really understand why I was feeling sexual love for my best friend. The line disappeared between friendship love and love that a girl would have for her boyfriend. Those feelings just seemed to intermesh. I wanted to tell her, but of course I was scared. A part of me believed that she would understand, being that she understood everything else I told her. I didn't want to ruin my relationship with my best friend, however. The confusion overwhelmed me. I didn't want to feel that way, but I just did and there was nothing I could do about it. One day I decided to tell her about my feelings.

"Can we talk about something?" I asked her.

"Sure," she said "Well, I don't know how to say what I want to say."

"It's okay, Autumn. Just say it."

After a few minutes of struggling with whether or not I should really go through with it, I just went ahead and let it all out.

"I feel like I am in love with you," I said timidly. Embarrassed and uneasy about what I just said, I started to cry. She embraced me and let me know she loved me.

"Don't cry, Autumn. Even though I don't feel the same way, I still love you. You are my best friend no matter what."

From that moment forward, our friendship took a turn. The covers had been pulled off what was really going on inside my heart, and now I had nothing to hide.

As time went on, my feelings continued and even increased. Soon after my confession, we began to experiment sexually. This was a confusing time for both of us, being that neither of us had ever done anything like this before. We remained best friends and had sexual experiences every once in a while. Both of us still had sexual experiences with different young men. I rode an emotional roller coaster in this season. I felt like I was in love with my best friend yet we had to keep it a big secret. My best friend sent me mixed messages. Despite saying that she did not share the same feelings for me, every once in a while she participated in these sexual encounters.

BREAKING ALL THE RULES

During my first year in college I had sexual intercourse with a young man who lived across the street from me. He was a few years younger than me and a virgin. This is why I think that I trusted him enough to allow him to have his way with me. We only had intercourse once before he moved. His Christian parents did not care for me too much because of the bad influence I exerted on their son.

I encouraged him to sneak out of the house late at night, when I came home from partying. He came to my house and then snuck back into his bedroom. His parents kept him in church, but I was not the type of girl they wanted him to marry. Since him I have had many sexual encounters with men, but not actual intercourse.

Throughout all of this my best friend met my need for love, support, safety, and concern. She filled a void in my heart. I had the safety of a friend and what I twisted into the love of a mother, coupled with a perverted lust. A homosexual spirit was trying to take over my life. I didn't have many sexual experiences with my best friend, but it opened the door for a whole new level of lust and perversion in my life.

By the age of twenty, I became pretty good friends with a girl I played basketball with in community college. I began to have sexual feelings for her. On a night that both of us had been drinking heavily, she kissed me.

"Oh my God!" she said as she pulled her face away from mine and covered her head under the blanket. "What am I doing?"

"What?" I said, questioning why she was freaking out.

"I just kissed a girl!" she said matter of factly.

"So what?" I said, reassuring her that it was okay.

For the first few times awkwardness hung between us because she had never done anything sexual with women before. It wasn't long, however, before we were fully engaged in a monogamous sexual relationship.

This relationship was nothing like what happened with my best friend. We began to engage in sexual activities on a much deeper level very quickly. I was filled with lust, and the homosexual spirit began to rule my life. I dressed more like a man than I had before, and my thoughts were filled with lust. I even went to adult bookstores to buy things to "spice up" our sex life. I was living in a whole new dimension of perversion, doing things that I never thought that I would do with women.

SHAME AND SECRECY

All the while I kept this a secret, or at least I thought I was. I was so ashamed of what I was doing. I was able to tell my friend whom I lived with in high school. But she was safe to tell. While I was still living in her parents' home my senior year in high school, she had started college and had moved into a dormitory. She met another female, and they became intimate. Then they developed a lesbian relationship. She had come home to visit her family and later on that night confessed to me that she was gay. This was before I had any sexual experiences with a female. She was crying and seemed so ashamed.

"It's okay," I assured her.

"Do you still love me?" she asked.

"Of course, I do. This doesn't change anything." I comforted her and let her know that she was still my friend and it didn't change my feelings for her. She proceeded to tell me that she had been hanging out at a gay bar in the Hillcrest area.

"Really?" I said. "Well, if you ever want me to go with you, I will," I told her in an attempt to let her know that I was serious about supporting her.

At age seventeen, with the same fake ID I used to get into clubs in Tijuana, I went with her to that gay bar.

"Stay close to me because I don't want any females hitting on me," I told her. She looked at me and smiled. "I'm serious," I told her.

Despite my discomfort, after a couple drinks I loosened up. I spent most of the night drinking and dancing by myself or with my friend. I went with her a few times and hung out. When approached by other women, I let them know that I was "straight."

COMING OUT

About six months later, when I started having feelings for my best friend in high school, I confided in the girl with whom I went to the gay bar because I knew that she would understand. When I later became involved in the lesbian relationship in college, she was the one whom I told. I still had three very close friends (which included the first female that I had sexual relations with in the past) from whom I hid the lesbian relationship for eight months. I was too ashamed to tell them, but I was too tied into it to let it go.

Eight months into my relationship with the female on the basketball team, I finally decided to tell my friends. When I told them, they already knew anyway. They just weren't saying anything to me. I spent all my time with this girl, and I came to class with hickies on my neck but wasn't talking about any man in my life. They knew and accepted it. They let me know that it didn't change the way they felt for me . . . and to be honest, it didn't. They never treated me any differently.

One day I remember driving in a car with another friend of mine whom I grew up with. Somehow the subject came up about me and the lifestyle I had been living.

"Men are no longer a challenge," I said arrogantly.

"Shut up," she said with a snicker.

"No, really," I said. "It's different with women; it's not as easy."

Some kind of false pride came with the fact that the two women that I had been with had never been with any other woman but me. Like I had some kind of power to turn women out and enjoyed the challenge of doing so. What I didn't realize is that the devil is in the soul winning business too, and he was using me for the purpose of building his kingdom.

Nine months into this relationship with the female I had played basketball with in college, I decided to tell my mom. This was the hardest thing for me to do. But I broke down and told her. I was crying and she was crying. I was embarrassed and ashamed of the fact that I had just revealed to my mother that the girl whom she thought was a really good friend of mine was really my girlfriend.

"I don't want you to go to hell!" my mom said, bursting into tears.

She proceeded to tell me that she still loved me. Of course, like everyone else, she already had her suspicions before I told her. I guess I wasn't hiding it as well as I thought I was. My female partner, on the other hand, refused to tell anyone that she was involved in a lesbian relationship. She had a whole lot of shame but continued to pursue her relationship with me.

We later began hanging out with another lesbian couple and could sometimes be found at the female gay bar in Hillcrest. I had gone there with my other friend when I was seventeen. I was still under the legal age to be in a bar, I might add. This was the only place that I felt somewhat comfortable showing my affection for my girlfriend in a place among many people whom I didn't know.

LIVING IN DENIAL

After I completed my units in community college, I was accepted into Cal State University Long Beach. I wanted to move and get away from the fast life that I lived in San Diego and focus on school. Still in the lesbian relationship, I asked my girlfriend if she wanted to move with me to Long Beach. She said she did. She would continue community college in Long Beach, and I would start at the university.

We remained in this relationship in Long Beach for another year and a half. We lived in a one bedroom townhouse. We had two beds to hide our relationship from people who didn't know. Throughout this time I still refused to classify myself as a lesbian. I surely never used the word "gay" to describe myself. Even though I was living the lifestyle, because I never lost my physical attraction for men, I believed that these terms did not describe me.

I don't remember even using the term bisexual to describe myself. I said that I could "go both ways." My sin had deceived me, and I was in denial.

I also carried a lot of shame about living as a lesbian. I was not comfortable being open with many people about my lifestyle. I certainly didn't parade it in public. The most public that I got was in the confines of a gay bar. My shame and guilt were making me sick inside. When I had severe stomach problems, my doctors ran many tests but found nothing specific. They linked my symptoms to stress. That is exactly what it was.

Living contrary to God's design stressed me out so much that I made myself sick inside. My mind continually raced, and I couldn't think straight. I had difficulty falling asleep at night. I used marijuana to relax. No matter what I did to numb myself, I had no real peace in my life.

3. Divine Intervention

One weekend I came down to San Diego and stayed with my mom and my stepfather. I often came home on weekends to hang out with my best friends and go clubbin'. On Sundays my mom asked, "Autumn, do you want to go to church?" Depending on how hung over I was, sometimes I went. I tried to go to support my mom.

This particular Sunday I decided to attend and invited one of my best friends to go with me. The awesome service made me feel like the message was just for me. During the altar call, my friend and I went to the altar. People formed a small circle around us and began to pray. I broke down and wept. The Lord began ministering to me in ways that I cannot verbalize. I left church that day not quite sure what really happened, but I knew that a change had occurred on the inside.

BREAKING IT OFF

Later that day, while lying on my mom's bed, I began to cry. "Mom," I whimpered, "I don't think that I am in love anymore. I don't think that I can do this anymore."

"Then you have to tell her, Autumn," my mom said.

I was ready to break it off. During the drive back to Long Beach, I told my girlfriend.

"I need to talk to you," I said.

"What's wrong?"

"I don't think I can do this anymore," I said.

"What do you mean?"

"I mean I don't think I can be with you anymore."

Silence filled the car as my girlfriend pulled off the freeway and stopped on the side of a road.

"Why? What happened? What did I do?" she asked as she began to cry.

"Nothing," I replied. "You didn't do anything. It's me. Something has changed in me. I don't know what's happening to me, but I just know that I can't do this anymore. "I was crying and feeling confused. We sat there for a while engaged in an emotion-filled tornado. Then we drove home in silence. By the time we arrived at our apartment in Long Beach, I had changed my mind and told her I didn't mean what I said. By the next day, however, I was sure again that I wanted out. After I ended the relationship, we had two sexual encounters. After that, I was through.

We continued to live together, in a one bedroom apartment, for the next six months until I graduated from college, but our relationship as lovers was over. Throughout those next six months, I knew that something had happened inside of me that day at church. I began coming home frequently on the weekends and attended church on most Sundays.

CHANGE BEGINS

Although I still had the desire for sex with a woman, I didn't act it out. I even shared with a friend that I probably would, if given the opportunity, have three-way sex with another female and male. I also shared with a few friends that I would never engage in sex with a woman again because I didn't want to go to hell. A battled raged inside of me. A war for my soul was being fought.

I remained physically attracted to men but still continued to view them as a means to an end. I could get my desires met without satisfying theirs through penetration. I spent a lot of time clubbin' with my friends and continued to drink heavily. When I graduated from college and moved back to San Diego, this cycle continued. I began to attend church more often with my mom, and the Lord was working in my heart.

Right around this time my mother hit me with bad news. She had just hung up the phone and came straight to my room. "Autumn," she cried in a quivering whimper. Immediately I knew something was wrong. She threw her arms around me. "I have breast cancer," she cried. My legs almost gave from underneath me.

What? I don't understand what that means, Mom. What does that mean?" I mumbled in a state of confusion that seemed to invade my world.

"I have cancer," she said again in a shaken voice.

I didn't know what to say. I didn't know what to do. I felt paralyzed with fear. I had just gotten my mom back, and now all I could think about was her dying. It felt so unfair. I didn't understand why this was happening to us. I continued to turn to alcohol and marijuana. I had only begun to know God's character. If my mother was going to survive cancer, I realized it would take an act of God. My mother later had a successful surgery and was completely healed by the hand of the Lord.

I began to get a little more serious about God. My faith began to increase. When I got high, I talked about spiritual things. All my friends said that I was deep. But something was happening on the inside of me. I seemed to be on the outside of my social circle looking in. I felt different.

I started making commitments to God like I wasn't going to drink or smoke on Sundays because it was a holy day. Later I tried to stop drinking and smoking by midnight on Saturday because technically that was Sunday. The closer it got to midnight, the faster I would drink to get in as much as I could before the clock struck midnight. Pretty sad, I know, but God was working on me. Most of the time I was able to keep these commitments. When I didn't, I felt guilty inside. If something bad happened, I linked it to the fact that I didn't keep my commitment to God.

GOD'S PROTECTION

One night while hanging out with my three best friends, the girls decided that they wanted to go to this club.

"I don't want to go," I said.

"Yeah you do. Come on, let's get up and get ready."

"I don't want to go," I said again.

This was unusual for me because I was always ready to go to the club. But this night I really didn't want to go for some reason. Content to just hang out at my friend's house, I wanted to drink a few beers. My friends insisted that we go, however. I don't know how many times I said I didn't want to go, but eventually I gave in.

We got ready, hopped in my jeep, and were on our way. While driving my jeep, I accepted a clove cigarette from my friend. I held it between my lips and leaned toward the passenger seat so that she could light it for me. When I looked up, I saw two headlights coming straight at us. I immediately yanked the wheel to the right, and the car missed us. My heart pounded so hard, it felt like it was going to burst through my chest. The car had gone down the wrong side of the freeway and just barely missed us. All of us freaked out on how close a call that was.

When we arrived at the club, I said, "We're going to pray before we go in this club. Grab hands." I prayed out loud and thanked God for sparing our lives. One of my friends, who experienced this near miss, attended church with me the next day. I stood up and testified about how the Lord had intervened on our behalf.

4. CLOSE ENCOUNTERS OF THE DEMON KIND

Not too long after that I had another strange encounter while at a club downtown with some friends. I was upstairs on the balcony drinking and leaning on the railing. I looked down below me and saw this guy leaning against a pole by the bar. He definitely caught my eye. He was so fine. Everything about his appearance attracted me. I couldn't keep my eyes off him.

I leaned over and nudged my friend. "Hey," I said. "Look at him, girl." She agreed that he was looking very good. A short while later, another guy approached me. "You wanna dance?" "All right," I said as I took his hand. As he led me downstairs, we began heading for the dance floor.

We had to pass the fine guy, who still stood by the pole, to get to the dance floor. As I walked past him, I felt a sudden urge to turn around and approach him. It felt like a magnetic force pulling me toward him. I let go of my escort's hand, turned around, and walked over to him.

"I just want to let you know that you are one beautiful-looking man," I said in his ear while I grabbed his hand. He smiled. I let go of his hand, walked away, and danced with the other guy.

Throughout the entire night the fine guy stood by that pole. I didn't see him talk to anyone or even drink any alcohol. He just stood there all night long. I kept my eye on him the entire evening. As it approached the club's closing time, my friends and I stood outside. Who started coming my way but the fine guy?

"How you doin'?" he asked.

"Fine. How are you?" I responded.

"Good," he said. "A friend and I drove here from Temecula to come to the club."

"Really? That's a long drive just to come to this club."

"Who are you here with?" he asked.

I pointed out my best friends.

"We're getting ready to go around the corner and pick up some weed. Then we're going back to my house. You and your friend can come if you want," I said.

"All right," he agreed. "We'll follow you."

Later at my house, we talked. My three friends talked with his friend, who rolled the weed. The fine guy and I got into a conversation about a Denzel Washington movie that was out at the time called *Fallen*. This movie depicts the transference of spirits through any type of physical contact. After we got deep into this conversation, he looked me in the eye and said, "I never saw the movie." I thought, *Okay, we just had this deep conversation about this movie, he talked to me in detail, yet he never saw the movie. Weird!* This was kind of odd, but I just blew it off.

Later the guy got up and sat by himself, on the floor, near a corner in the living room. He got extremely quiet. Now I have smoked some potent weed, but this was not, so I was kind of trippin' about how he was acting.

"You have a sweatshirt I can wear? I'm cold," he said softly with his arms folded across his knees, which were pulled up to his chest. I lived in a small apartment, and it was not cold at all, but I gave him a big Adidas sweatshirt to wear. He put it on, folded his arms on his knees, and put his head down.

I thought, Now he's about to pass out.

A few minutes later the guy lifted his head, turned it toward me, and looked me in the eyes. As I returned his gaze, I immediately noticed that his eyes looked weird. As I looked closer, I realized that his eyes had turned a bright silver-gray color. He then slowly put his head back down. I was shocked at what I had just seen and started getting scared. I hit my friend in the leg and whispered in her ear, "Oh, my God! His eyes are changing colors!"

"What?" she asked.

"His eyes just changed colors!"

"Girl, you're trippin!"

"No! I'm serious! He just lifted up his head, looked at me, and his eyes were silver. I'm not playin'. Watch," I said.

A couple minutes later the guy slowly lifted his head, turned very slowly, and stared directly into my eyes with his silver eyes, and then put his head back down.

"Tell me you didn't see that?" I said. My friend claimed to have seen it but later confessed that she really didn't.

I had enough of this guy and wanted him out of my house.

"He's got to go," I told my friend. "I'm not playin'. He's got to go now!"

One of my friends announced, "Hey, we're hungry. Let's get something to eat."

Needless to say, the guy with the funny eyes stayed put and didn't budge an inch. My friend continued to announce that we wanted to leave. The guy's friend then said, "You guys act like we're trying to put a curse on you or something."

What! These guys need to get up and out of my house, I thought. Finally, the silver-eyed guy got up and went to my bathroom without saying a word. I had my friend watch him and see that he didn't go into my bedroom.

"Don't let him go into my bedroom. I don't want him in my room!" I told her.

He went into the bathroom, came back out, handed me my sweatshirt, and walked out the door. We all walked out together, and my friends and I headed to the taco shop.

While in the drive-thru, I started talking to my friends about what I had seen.

"Did you guys see his eyes? They turned silver. He was just sitting there and then looked up at me, and his eyes were silver! I think he was the devil or something!"

I was so shook up about the whole thing that I began to cry. I was the only one in the room who had seen everything that happened. My friends saw the guy's weird behavior, but I was the only one who saw what I believed to be "the devil." My eyes were immediately opened to the sequence of events that happened that night.

The devil knows exactly what I am attracted to, so he set up this guy in the club. I felt a strong drawing toward him. The enemy of my soul stationed him at the club for me. That's why he wasn't interacting with anyone else. Then we spoke about the movie *Fallen,* which is about the transference of spirits. Having never seen the movie, he sure knew a lot about the transference of spirits. I instantly linked this to what the devil wanted to do through this guy. He wanted to transfer that wicked spirit to me.

What if I would have had sex with him? I thought. That spirit would have transferred directly into me. I became so frightened. God showed me all that the devil had planned for me that evening. I rambled on to my friends the sequence of events that happened. They pacified me by listening intently. I got home with my tacos and told one of my friends to spend the night with me because I was scared. I bit into my taco, immediately realized that I had not "blessed" my food, and quickly dropped my taco.

"What is going on?" I said frantically. I instantly picked up the phone and called my mom. It was around 4:00 a.m. when my mom's phone rang.

"Hello," my mom said in a sleepy voice.

"Mom," I whimpered.

"Autumn, what's wrong?" my mom asked, detecting the panic in my voice.

"Mom, the devil is trying to get me!"

"What?"

"I just saw the devil, and he wanted to get me!" I told my mom all that happened. "Mom, can you please pray for me?" I asked.

My mother prayed for me over the phone that night. As I went to bed, I could not stop thinking about what had happened. I was petrified.

The next evening while at work I went into a Christian chat room and shared this experience with a woman. The woman began to minister to me. "You must be the apple of God's eye because the devil does not just manifest himself like that to everyone," she wrote. "The Lord must really have plans for your life." I wrote down everything that this woman ministered to me. I was so relieved in knowing that someone really believed me.

This experience was as real to me today as it was then. Many people just write it off and say that I just smoked a little too much that night. But I know what I saw that night. Seeing his eyes change color blew my high. I was completely sober after that. These experiences woke me up to the fact that the devil is real and that God wanted to do something in my life. The devil knows that his time is short. He tried to kill me while he had the chance. He targeted me while I was living in his territory. But the hand of the Lord was upon my life. Even in my rebellion the Lord covered me.

"ONE YEAR FROM TODAY"

About a month later, after a late night of partying, I came to church with a major hangover. I had passed out at a friend's house after throwing up the night before. The following day she woke me up. "Aren't you going to church?" she asked. I stumbled out of the sleeper sofa and headed for the shower. I threw on a pair of my friend's jeans and made it to church that day. Looking back, I probably reeked of alcohol.

While at church, the Lord ministered to me in such a powerful way. I ended up at the altar where the speaker, Elder Dion Reid, prophesied to me, "One year from today you will not even recognize the person who is standing here." The Lord was getting ready to turn my life around.

From that day forward, everything began to change. I spoke with my pastor about my struggle with lesbianism. He really helped me to understand why and how I was even tempted to participate in that lifestyle. He talked to me about the love that I had for my mother, the longing for a mother figure, and the void that I was trying to fill.

I know that ultimately I had sex with who I wanted to have sex with, and I cannot blame this on anyone but myself. I also know that some basic underlying needs in my life were not addressed in my childhood. These conversations with my pastor released me into a whole new realm in my spiritual walk. Not only had I gained understanding about myself, but at the same time I felt comfortable enough to share my deepest secrets with a man. I learned that my pastor was a man of God whom I could trust. The healing process began with those sessions.

Within a month of the prophetic word spoken over my life, I wasn't drinking, smoking, or having any kind of sex. I began to seriously search the Scriptures, pray, and attend church services— even during the week. I no longer desired to go to the clubs, and I made my friends aware of that. I began to separate myself from people who didn't want to go in my direction. This was difficult, and I spent many nights crying myself to sleep as I talked to the Lord. I knew that the very people whom I had grown so attached to were the very ones whom I had to let go. The Lord truly was working a work in my life. I felt so free and I had never felt such peace. All I wanted to do was get to know my newfound friend, Jesus Christ.

FROM DARKNESS TO LIGHT

Shortly after my salvation I contacted the girl with whom I had I lived in Long Beach and had a long-term sexual relationship.

"Hey, how are you doin?" I asked. We engaged in small talk briefly. "You want to go to church with me on Sunday?"

"Sure," she said. At church that day, my ex-lesbian lover went to the altar and gave her heart to Jesus. When I drove her home, I spoke candidly and openly with her about the changes that God had made in my life.

"Yeah, God has done an awesome work in my life," I told her. "And I want you to know that everything that we did together was wrong. It was sin."

I shared with her how God feels about these things. This conversation and the conversion that God made happen were so awesome. Praise God that the soul that I had converted to the kingdom of darkness had now been converted to the kingdom of light.

When Jesus saved me, the spirit of homosexuality had to loose me. That spirit no longer ruled my life. It no longer had dominion over me. I had been given the power to overcome it and to move forward in my relationship with Jesus. Little did I know that I still needed to be fully delivered from the layers of residue that had been left behind.

As I went through my belongings, I began to do some spring cleaning. I got rid of things that reminded me of my past lifestyle—jewelry, clothes, photographs, and gifts from the lesbian relationship. I either gave away or trashed many of these belongings. I wanted nothing to connect me to that lifestyle. This was one of the first steps in my transition. Little did I know that a whole lot of spring cleaning still needed to happen on the inside.

5. DELIVERED OR DELIVERED?

As I searched the Scriptures, I came across this verse: "I removed his shoulder from the burden: his hands were delivered from the pots" (Ps. 81:6). Meditating on its meaning led me to do a word study.

This word **"delivered"** means: *cross over or transition*. That is exactly what God did for me. He caused me to cross over. He transitioned me out of a place of sin and brought me into a safe haven. He drew me into His arms and brought me into a church where I was surrounded by people who loved me. They wanted nothing more than to see me grow in the Lord. At this stage in my life, I was "delivered" in this sense of the word. God had caused me to cross over from a lifestyle of lust-ridden partying, from a tormented existence, to a place of safety in the arms of the Lord.

Verse 7 of this psalm reads: "Thou calledst in trouble, and I delivered thee." This word **"delivered"** comes from the Hebrew word *chalats* and means: *to pull off; to strip; to depart; to equip for fight; present; strengthen*. This stripping and pulling off can be a painful process. It is a necessary process, however. It is to deliver you. It is to equip you for the fight. It is to strengthen you. If you can make it through the process, you can make it through the storms that come with being a Christian. This is the process of deliverance that I would come to know for myself.

For my first two years of salvation, I went forth in the Lord. I continued to learn more and more about my newfound friend, Jesus Christ. I attended church regularly, read and studied the Bible, and began to have a prayer life. I started fasting and witnessing to people. My faith was strong. I even began working in the house of the Lord. The church body that the Lord placed me in was full of love and compassion. I had never felt such love and acceptance.

GODLY COMPANIONS

The people in this church had come from the same type of life that my mother and I had lived. Many church members had come out of prison, addictions, and all types of bondage. These people were real and talked freely about their feelings and what they were going through. I saw such an openness and concern for one another. Most of all, the ministers preached the uncompromising Word of God. The people spoke truth into my life. I had, and still have today, pastors after God's own heart. My pastors will not only nurture and love but will also rebuke and correct when needed. I thank God today for The Fellowship of Love Divine.

God also gave me new friendships in the Lord. I found I had many brothers and sisters in Christ. One sister, who was and still is a mentor to me, took me under her wing, She was someone whom I could look up to and communicate with. She demonstrated what a true woman of God should be. To this day she is still my sister, my friend, my mentor, and an example for me.

In the early stages of our relationship, however, I was hesitant to get too close to her because I didn't want my feelings to suddenly switch on me. I desperately wanted to believe that homosexuality was no longer a part of me and that I could be close with *all* women without developing sexual feelings for them. In the past, I had a lot of female friends, but not all were healthy relationships.

Two years into my relationship with the Lord, I went to a Christian conference in Tulsa, Oklahoma, where Pastor Donnie McClurkin testified of his deliverance from homosexuality. At the end of his message he told people to come to the altar if they were dealing with issues in their sexuality. While I stood at my seat, the Holy Spirit began to prompt me to go to the altar. I wrestled with the Holy Ghost and argued in my mind that homosexuality was no longer my issue. I hadn't had sex with a woman in over three years. I had been saved for two years now. I struggled with the thought of having all of the people with whom I went to the conference look at me and say, "I knew she wasn't delivered." But I knew I needed to go to that altar. Despite being saved and filled with the Holy Ghost, I needed that altar that day. As I took those steps to the altar, the process of deliverance began.

6. Exposure and Identification

The day that I went to the altar in Tulsa, Oklahoma, my process of deliverance from homosexuality began. The Holy Ghost revealed to me that issues of homosexuality still existed deep below the surface of my Christianity. They had not been totally dealt with. Although I struggled to admit it, these issues were still alive and needed to be processed out.

I had been running and trying to hide from it. I desperately wanted to believe that I no longer had these issues. I hadn't participated in any homosexual activity in over three years. Although the fruit of that lifestyle wasn't seen, the roots lay beneath the surface. With God's help, I needed to pull them out. The grace of God appeared to reveal these issues and help me through the process.

"MY GRACE IS SUFFICIENT"

In order to have true deliverance, you must have the courage to face the issues of your life that the Holy Ghost brings to your awareness. When the Lord shines His divine, holy light on your issue, it is time to deal with it. Why? Because the grace of God is there for you to deal with it at this time. Many issues will remain covered until you are strengthened in your faith. Then the Holy Ghost will help you deal with them. If the Lord reveals an issue in your life, His grace is there to strengthen you in your moment of weakness. He is there to help you to overcome that issue. If God showed you all of your issues on the day that you got saved, you would be so overwhelmed, you would probably backslide. He allows those areas to be hidden from you until your relationship with Him is strengthened. Then He begins to give you revelation of yourself.

When the apostle Paul dealt with his thorn in his flesh, Jesus told him, "My grace is sufficient for thee: for my strength is made perfect in weakness" (2 Cor. 12:9). Paul responded, "Most gladly therefore would I rather glory in my infirmities, that the power of Christ may rest upon me." Did Paul get discouraged about his infirmities? No. He declared that he would glory in his infirmities that the power of Christ would rest upon him. Paul knew that if he gave God glory in the midst of his battle, ultimately the power of Christ would rest upon him. He knew that even in his struggle, he was going to come out with some power. What an example for us to follow.

The Holy Spirit is the friend of every Christian. Jesus comforted His disciples by telling them, "Howbeit when he, the Spirit of truth is come, he will guide you into all truth" (John 16:7). The Holy Ghost, your friend, will come to show you the truth about yourself. You will see the raw, undiluted, unsugar-coated truth about who you are on the inside. He doesn't do this to overwhelm you with guilt. The Holy Ghost does not come to condemn you. The Holy Ghost knows that at the other end of this battle, a greater anointing is on reserve for you. If you just get to the other side of this road, the Lord will heal you and use you to bring healing in the lives of others.

HOW DOES GOD SPEAK?

The Holy Spirit can and will speak to you in many different ways. He helped me to identify and process issues related to homosexuality. I heard the testimony of Pastor Donnie McClurkin, which was interwoven with the preached Word of God. Hearing the Word of God taught from the pulpit is a common way that the Holy Spirit speaks to many of us. Testimonies are also a method that the Holy Spirit uses.

Many people are moved upon by the Holy Spirit while they sit in church services. Although they are convicted by the Spirit of

Truth, as soon as they leave the church, the seed of righteousness that has been planted in their spirit is choked out. Although they may have come to the altar and even received the laying on of hands, these people leave church without making any kind of commitment to follow up and process out the issue that God brought to their attention. Because of this, many Christians receive what I would call a surface deliverance.

With makeup smeared on their face and dried up tears, they tell you that the Lord delivered them today. Now the Lord very well may have delivered them today. He is able to do it in a flash. But my experience has been that when you have deep-seated issues, your deliverance is a process. Although mighty things happen in your spirit in church services, I believe there is usually a process that you have to be willing to walk out. That process begins when you leave church that day.

> But be ye doers of the word and not hearers only, deceiving your own selves. For if any be a hearer of the word, and not a doer, he is like unto a man beholding his natural face in a glass: For he beholdeth himself, and goeth his way, and straightway forgetteth what manner of man he was. (James 1:22–24)

Hearing the Word identifies and exposes the issue, but we must do some work in our lives outside of the church building.

Another way that the Holy Spirit may speak to you is through His written Word. "But whoso looketh into the perfect law of liberty, and continueth therein, he being not a forgetful hearer, but a doer of the work, this man shall be blessed in his deed" (James 1:25). It is an absolute necessity for Christians to spend time in the Word of God for themselves. The Holy Ghost can take His Word and reveal truth in you like you have never known truth before.

Every Scripture is God breathed (given by His inspiration) and profitable for instruction, for reproof and conviction of sin, for correction of error and discipline in obedience, [and] for training in righteousness (in holy living, in conformity to God's will in thought, purpose, and action) So that the man of God may be complete and proficient, well fitted and thoroughly equipped for every good work. (2 Tim. 3:16–17 AMP)

The Word of God is a mirror for us. As our standard for holy living, it shows us where we fall short of that standard. Then the Holy Ghost can help make us complete, equipped, and ready to be used. Once we see the Word and accept it as truth for our lives, we must allow the Word of God to work its work on the inside of us. It will cleanse and purify us on the inside from everything that is not like God. This is all a part of the process. We must read and study the Word of God ourselves for truth to be revealed and the issues in our lives to be identified and exposed.

The Holy Spirit will also expose you to yourself in the inner sanctums of prayer. In prayer the light of God's holiness shines on you and reveals what you look like to Him. This can be a very humbling experience. When the prophet Isaiah got into the presence of the Lord, how did he react? He cried out, "Woe is me! For I am undone; because I am a man of unclean lips, and I dwell in the midst of a people of unclean lips: for mine eyes have seen the King, the Lord of hosts" (Isa. 6:5).

During times of prayer the Holy Ghost will begin to minister to you about issues that need work. During this time issues can be exposed, identified, and dealt with. Why is prayer so necessary for every Christian? It not only reveals to us our true character but it also allows us to begin to discern the voice of the Holy Spirit.

WHAT'S HIDDEN IN YOUR HEART?

We have to get down to the nitty gritty, to open our eyes to the truth that we need to be delivered. David said, "Behold, thou desirest truth in the inward parts: and in the hidden part thou shalt make me to know wisdom" (Ps. 51:6). This entire psalm is a cry of confession and repentance to the Lord.

David had committed the sin of adultery with Bathsheba and then conspired to have Uriah, Bathsheba's husband, killed. The Lord then sent Nathan, a prophet, to tell David the consequences of his sin. This psalm was written out of David's anguish. He accepted his responsibility for the sin that he had committed. He also surrendered to the Lord for purification of everything in his spirit that was not like God.

David recognized that he had some issues that needed to be dealt with. The sins that he had committed were just an outward manifestation of the issues that were hidden in the inner recesses of his heart. When the word of the Lord came to David and revealed sin in his life, David confessed his sin.

And David said unto Nathan, I have sinned against the Lord. (2 Sam. 12:13)

Wash me thoroughly from mine iniquity, and cleanse me from my sin. For I acknowledge my transgressions: and my sin is ever before me. Against thee, thee only, have I sinned and done this evil in thy sight: that thou mightest be justified when thou speakest, and be clear when thou judgest. (Ps. 51:2–4)

Notice that David did not just stop with admission and confession. He acknowledged that something needed to happen in his heart and spirit for the process of deliverance to be completed. "Create in me a clean heart, O God; and renew a right spirit within me" (Ps. 51:10). David looked into the inner sanctums of his heart and wanted to be cleansed from everything that was not like God. He prayed, "Purge me with hyssop and I shall be clean; wash me, and I shall be whiter than snow" (v. 7). David was not afraid to look at himself and to deal with the issues at hand. When the Lord revealed truth to him, he saw himself clearly, repented, and went back to God with his issues, knowing that God has the power to heal and to restore.

HINDRANCES TO HEARING

In order to identify issues in our life, we must hear from the Holy Spirit. The Spirit of God will bring you into truth about an issue that He is ready to help you work on, but you have to be in a place to hear the Spirit. You also have to be humble enough to admit that the issue exists.

People cannot hear from the Holy Spirit for many reasons. Early in our Christian walk we often cannot discern the voice of the Holy Spirit because we have not spent enough time in fellowship with Him yet. We learn to discern the voice of the Holy Ghost through prayer and communion with Him. As we spend more time with Him, we begin to learn what His voice sounds like.

People also may not hear the voice of the Holy Ghost because they have so many other voices constantly speaking to them. As a believer you must watch who influences you. Surrounding yourself with the wrong people hinders your ability to hear from the Spirit of God. You also need to guard the gateway to your soul. Your gates include your eyes, ears, and mouth. Be cautious about what you allow to come in and out of your spirit.

Un-confessed sin hinders us from hearing the Holy Spirit with clarity. When we carry un-confessed sin in our lives, it is difficult to hear what the Lord speaks to us regarding other issues in our heart. I believe David—the man after God's own heart—was not able to hear the Spirit of God for himself because of un-confessed sin. I believe this is why the Lord sent Nathan the prophet to speak into his life.

GETTING YOUR ATTENTION

If you refuse to allow the Spirit of God to deal with you about your issues, God will send people in your life to help you identify your issues. The Holy Ghost will not expose your issues to other people just for the sake of exposing you. He always tries to get your attention first. He desires intimacy with you. Intimacy involves a private place of communion between you and the Holy Spirit. If you refuse to allow the Holy Spirit to show you an issue, and you refuse to accept and identify the issue as your own, then He will send a seer into your life to show you yourself.

The word seer comes from the Hebrew word *ro'eh,* which means: *a visionary, one who sees visions; a prophet. Ro'eh* comes from the verb *ra'ah,* which means: *"to see,"* but also has a wide range of meanings relating to seeing (such as *"perceive, appear, discern, look, stare"*). Seers are necessary in the life of every believer.

Soon after our conversion, most of us are not really able to discern the voice of the Holy Ghost or identify areas in our lives that could be dangerous to us if there is not some immediate resolution. The Lord will place people around you who will be able to see into certain areas of your life. The Lord will give them insight regarding what you need to go to the next level. Seers not only see into certain areas of your life that need to be worked on, but also see beyond your current situations, circumstances, and character defects. These visionaries see you in your future, going forth in the calling that God has placed upon your life.

I praise God for every seer that the Lord has placed in my life. Pastors have been called to shepherd and watch over the sheep. Many times I couldn't see the potential dangers in certain situations. In my own personal time with the Lord, I neglected or refused to look at the risk factors that were involved. But the Lord placed pastors in my life that saw into and beyond the current situations. Seers will show you potential dangers that you may be blinded to because of neglect, denial, or just the inability to hear from the Holy Ghost. Seers are good.

Although I firmly believe that people need to seek the Lord for themselves, I am also convinced that every Christian needs someone who has the ability to see into you when you cannot see into yourself. Some things in your life need to be identified. Our mindset has to be, "God, whatever You need to do to show me myself; whoever You need to use to bring me truth; Lord, You have Your way."

Identifying the issue in your life is necessary for beginning the walk down the road of process. If you deny that you have anything to work on, then the Lord, out of His love for you, will allow storms, situations, and circumstances to arise in your life to get your attention. Sometimes this is the only way that you will realize that you have work to do. Usually in the tough times we begin to truly turn to God. When there is no other way out, then we say, "OK, God. Here I am." And God says, "Finally! Now that I have your attention, let Me show you a few things about yourself."

Whatever you do when you're in the fire, don't throw more fuel on it by murmuring and complaining. Determine in your heart that you will get into the presence of the Lord and see what is really going on. It could just be that He has been trying to get you in His presence all along, so that He could show you a few things about yourself.

Somebody reading this right now has no idea why you are going through a particular trial. I dare you to take fifteen minutes, shut yourself in a room, and cry out to God. Take fifteen minutes and God will speak. You're frustrated, discontent, and depressed. You feel like you just want to throw in the towel and give up. You have no idea what is going on in your life.

The Lord is trying to get your attention. God wants to process out some areas in your life. He wants to purify other areas. He will show you that you have to release some people for a season. He sees greatness in you. He wants to use you. He has a plan to use you to save someone else.

Submit to Him today. Submit to Him right now. You will come out of this situation when you begin to take your eyes off your circumstance and place your eyes on Him. That's when He can show you yourself. When you come out, you will look back and understand why you were in the situation. You will see for yourself that you have grown, you have matured, and you have gained an anointing to go forth in the name of the Lord. Go through the process. Begin by getting in His presence. Allow Him to identify the issues that He wants to help you work on, and start today.

7. HATE WHAT GOD HATES

Do you want to be more like God? While reading the psalms, I came across a verse that described something about God's character that caused me to think. "Thou lovest righteousness, and hatest wickedness: therefore God, thy God, hath anointed thee above thy fellows" (Ps. 45:7). Does that describe you? Do you love what God loves and hate what God hates? I had begun to see my life from God's perspective, and my hatred for wickedness was growing.

Here I am, Lord, open to You. I'm naked and ashamed of what has been found residing in my heart. It has been there all the time. Gracious God, You allowed me to fall deeply in love with You before pulling back the covers on the issue of homosexuality that was still lodged in my spirit. I don't want it to be there. As a matter of fact, I have come to hate that it has been exposed in me. I don't want it there. I want more than anything to be freed from this issue. Where do I go from here?

This was the cry of my heart when the Lord revealed my issue and I identified it for what it truly was. Even though I had not engaged in any homosexual activity in over three years, and had been saved and serious about my relationship with Jesus Christ for two years, deep on the inside of me an issue needed to be uprooted. I began to hate this issue with a passion.

IS IT REALLY SIN?

If you believe that homosexuality is acceptable to God, please do not be deceived. The Bible makes it clear that homosexual activity is an abomination in the sight of the Lord. Both Old and New Testament passages confirm this. "Thou shalt not lie with mankind as with womankind: it is abomination" (Lev. 18:22).

The word abomination in this verse comes from the Hebrew word *toeda,* which interpreted is: *a detestable or loathsome thing.* To loathe something is to hate it. "If a man also lie with mankind, as he lieth with a woman, both of them hath committed an abomination: they shall surely be put to death; their blood shall be upon them" (Lev. 20:13).

> Do you not know that the unrighteous and the wrongdoers will not inherit or have any share in the kingdom of God? Do not be deceived (misled): neither the impure and immoral, nor idolaters, nor adulterers, nor those who *participate in homosexuality,* nor cheats (swindlers and thieves), nor greedy graspers, nor drunkards, nor foulmouthed revilers and slanderers, nor extortioners or robbers will inherit or have any share in the kingdom of God. (1 Cor. 6:9–10 AMP)

God hates the act of homosexuality. Participation in the act of homosexuality is sin. But thank God that He sent His Son Jesus Christ that we may receive grace, forgiveness, and cleansing from all of our sins.

COME TO JESUS

If you are battling homosexuality, you need to know that God loves you. He desires to save and deliver you. Do not allow yourself to get frustrated over how God feels about those who act out homosexual behavior. Do not put this book down and turn away from it in anger. That is what the enemy of your soul wants you to do. You can give your life to Christ right now and be filled with the power to overcome the bondage of that lifestyle. You can be given power over all the power of the enemy (See Luke 10:19). You can walk through the process and come out completely set free.

My friend, there is a peace in Jesus Christ that you will never find in any other relationship. In all your searching, Jesus has led you to this book, because he wants to come into your heart and reveal Himself to you in a way that you have never known Him before. Today is your day. Jesus stands at the door of your heart knocking. Let Him in by sincerely praying this prayer aloud now:

> *Jesus, I need You. I admit that I am a sinner and that I need to be forgiven for my sins. I believe that You died for me and that You rose from the grave. I confess You as my Lord and my Savior. Please save me and fill me with Your Holy Spirit. Empower me to overcome the snare of homosexuality. Break me free from its power today. I am willing to go through the process to receive complete and total deliverance from everything from my past that would try to hinder my walk with You. Thank You for the eternal gift of salvation. In Jesus' mighty name, amen.*

If you just prayed that prayer, then you are saved. The Lord Jesus Christ has just washed you clean from every sin you have ever committed. You are completely forgiven. Praise the Lord. The Lord is going to reveal Himself to you in a mighty way. You are now a part of the family of God. Thank You, Jesus. I encourage you to read the Bible, spend time with God in prayer, and begin attending church regularly. Oh yes, and continue reading the rest of this book!

God is love (1 John 4:8). It is not the Lord's will that any should perish but that all should come to repentance (2 Pet. 3:9). God is in love with people—all kinds of people. People who are gay. People who are straight. People who are on drugs. People who are rich. People who are poor. People who have committed murder. People who have molested children. God is so in love with people that He had His Son murdered that people could be forgiven for all of their sins.

God hates the act of sin. He despises the spirit of darkness. There is no big sin and little sin in the sight of God. All sin is sin, and that's just all sin is. "For all have sinned, and come short of the glory of God" (Rom. 3:23). "For the wages of sin is death, but the gift of God is eternal life through Jesus Christ our Lord" (Rom. 6:23). Everyone has sinned, and all of us need to receive the gift of eternal life through Jesus Christ in order to escape the debt for our sin, which is death. Praise God for Jesus Christ His Son.

RIDDING MYSELF OF RESIDUE

Even though I no longer participated in the act of homosexuality, residue from that lifestyle still remained inside me. Even though I knew that God loved me, I began to realize that He wanted to purge some things from me. His love for me never wavered. He knew that my heart was for Him. But He desired to process that junk out so that I could be more like Him. "This then is the message which we have heard of him, and declare unto you, that God is light, and in him is no darkness at all" (1 John 1:5).

Was I still saved even with this residue inside me? Yes, wholly and completely. But I had not been purified from the issues of homosexuality. Now was the time for the purification process to begin. God wanted to purge out those things inside of me that connected me to that lifestyle. As much as I declared out of my mouth that I would never participate in the homosexual lifestyle again, it would have been extremely dangerous for me to not allow the Lord to take me through the process of deliverance.

Even having been processed, I still must be sober, watchful, and alert. "Wherefore, let him that thinketh he standeth take heed lest he fall" (1 Cor. 10:12). In other words, even now I cannot become lazy and let my guard down. I know that the flesh will deceive you if you do not keep it in subjection. Even the apostle Paul knew this. He wrote, "But I keep under my body, and bring it into subjection: lest that by any means, when I have preached to others, I myself should be a castaway" (1 Cor. 9:27).

I have to watch myself. It is not good for me to watch sex scenes on the movie screen. I know that this opens a door in my mind for lustful thoughts to take root. A few days later, I may wonder why I have lustful thoughts. I will have to work to filter out those thoughts later. It is not worth the work. It is not worth the time. I have a responsibility to the anointing that is on my life to guard my mind. I must not forget that the issue of lust tried to kill me. Whether it was homosexual or heterosexual lust, lust is just lust. So I have to be aware of what I allow to come in to my mind. I cannot afford to give the enemy access or the flesh room to rise.

I must recognize there is a real enemy who would love to see me lose my testimony. He would love to see me back in bondage, held captive by the spirits of homosexuality and lust. He comes every once in a while to see if he can plant a bad seed in my mind. If I told you that I never had a lustful thought, since I have been through the process, I would be lying to you.

So what's the difference? Now these thoughts no longer live and dwell in my mind like they used to. These out-of-town visitors try to stop by every once in a while. They are foreigners and strangers and, therefore, very recognizable. I see these thoughts for what they are, and I know who is trying to plant them. I no longer own these thoughts because they are not mine. They do not belong to me. They come neatly wrapped, disguised as a gift that the enemy wants me to open. But I recognize his writing and write on them, "The old Autumn is no longer at this address. Return to sender."

Sometimes his tactics are laughable. But I still cannot afford to underestimate their potential for danger. Even though these thoughts are few and far between, I still must confront them before they take root. I cast down these thoughts before they are allowed to make themselves at home in my mind. The apostle Paul tells us what to do: "Casting down imaginations and every high thing that exalteth itself against the knowledge of God, and bringing into captivity every thought to the obedience of Christ" (2 Cor. 10:5).

I hope I haven't been so real here that I have scared some of you away. We must take responsibility for guarding our minds and maintaining our deliverance. Now back to the issues at hand.

HATE WHAT GOD HATES

Whatever your issue, you must develop a hatred for that thing. What do you struggle with? Is it lust, jealousy, envy, strife, anger, addiction, or depression? You must realize that that thing is inside you, and it desires to destroy you. You must admit that this issue is something that God hates because it can only lead to sin. There is no good in the issue itself. It is not like God and, therefore, you must develop a hatred for it. His hatred for the issue must become your hatred. We have to learn to hate what God hates. You must recognize that this issue is a tool that the enemy will use against you. If you don't deal with it, you give him an advantage over your soul.

You must develop hatred for the enemy of your soul, the issue in your spirit, and the lust of your flesh. When the enemy provokes you enough, when that thing in your flesh rises to a level that you know it could kill you or cause you to backslide, then you realize the need to deal with the issue. You sense and feel the danger of the issue at hand. You begin to develop a hatred for the issue because you know that it could spiritually murder you.

I don't know about you, but if someone tried to kill me, I would do everything I could to fight for my life. Kick, bite, yell, and scream, act crazy— whatever it took to escape with my life.

You must understand the need to develop hatred for the issue that is trying to take you out.

Hate is a strong word. My mother used to reprimand me for using the word hate. If I said that I hated a certain type of cereal, she automatically corrected me and told me that I didn't hate it; I just didn't like it. She taught me that hate was a very strong word to use to describe my feelings and should not be used lightly.

Many people in the Body of Christ suffer because leaders, brothers, and sisters have failed to take on the character of God to hate sin, wickedness, and ungodliness. God just doesn't "not like" sin. He hates it. We have settled for just "not liking" sin and ungodliness. We just "don't like" the fact that we struggle with lustful thoughts. The Bible describes how you should feel about the struggles in your mind: "I hate vain thoughts: but thy law do I love" (Ps. 119:113).

As a result the Church has become weak and accepting of things that we ought to stand against and hate. The things that we should love—like the Word of God, prayer, righteousness, and holiness—we settle for just "liking" rather than loving. If we loved righteousness and hated wickedness, no homosexuals would be playing the organ in our churches. There would be no fornicators in the choir. There would be no adulterous preachers behind the pulpit. There would be no more rebellious youth leaders transferring that spirit to our youth.

But instead the Church has allowed and accepted what she is supposed to hate and despise. Love the person but hate the sin. We must adopt an attitude of hatred toward those things inside us that try to work death in us. Many of us think that they are just a part of who we are. They always have been there and always will be there. Many have gotten so used to those issues that they have become comfortable with them being there.

Issues that we leave unchecked long enough will continue to gain strength and power. They will overtake you and have you enslaved in the chains of bondage. Issues left unchecked will open the door for the enemy to come in and begin to do damage. Soon you will be wondering why you cannot stay focused. Why your mind has been ravished with lustful thoughts. Why you do not have the desire to pray and read the Bible. You would rather be at home on the couch than in a church service. You have lost your joy. Peace has turned into torment. You have left your door open, and the enemy is your welcomed guest.

This is serious! You have to take authority over your life and declare to yourself and to the enemy that you love righteousness and hate everything inside you that is not like God. You have to get serious about your salvation and submit to the process of deliverance. You have to desire holiness and purification. You have to allow the Lord to refine you for His glory. The sooner you begin to deal with your issues, the better.

CHECK YOUR HEART

If all you want to do is be saved and slide into heaven on that great day, then this book may not be for you. Look at the attitude of your heart. Are you okay with just being saved, with just staying saved from Sunday to Sunday? Are you proud of yourself for just not committing any big sin for the week? Do you feel like you have done God a favor by staying saved? If you answered yes to any of those questions, then this book is probably not for you.

This book is for people who want to be delivered. It's for those who are so grateful that the Lord rescued them from the pit of hell that they will lay down their lives for the gospel's sake. This book is for people who want to go all the way with God. This book is for individuals who are tired of just playing church and really want to experience the power of God in their lives. This book is not for the average, everyday Christian.

Are you pursuing holiness, and do you want nothing more than to be conformed to His image? Do you want the Lord to get glory from your life? Are you so grateful that you just want to offer your life back to God so He can use you in the lives of others? Perhaps this is your heart's cry, yet you know some unresolved issues remain in your life. If you have some areas that need to be purged or purified—and you are willing to go through the process—my sister or brother, this book is for you!

Just submit yourself to the authority of God and allow Him to renew you in the spirit of your mind. You will begin to love what God loves (righteousness) and hate what God hates (wickedness). What is the result of identifying with God's affections? Your God will anoint you above your fellows (Ps. 45:7).

To God be the glory.

8. THE ISSUES OF LIFE

Many people in the church struggle with various issues. Whether they would be willing and open enough to share them with you is another matter. Some allow the process to take place while others refuse it. Do not let the enemy deceive you into believing that you are the only one in the church who struggles. Let's look at some of those issues that cause Christians to struggle.

IT STARTS IN THE HEART

Some of the greatest men and women of the Bible, even after they came to God, struggled. David had his battle with lust. Because he hadn't dealt with the issue in his heart, he committed adultery. He even had the women's husband killed so that he could have her to himself. David not only committed adultery, he also conspired to murder the husband.

All of this began with a look. David spotted Bathsheba bathing naked on the rooftop. If he had walked away, none of these events would have taken place. When David yielded to the lust of his flesh, what started as temptation turned into sin. Despite his failures, God called him "a man after [mine] own heart" (1 Sam. 13:14). Why? Because of his willingness to acknowledge his sin, repent, and move forward.

For Christians who have come out of the homosexual lifestyle, lust is the biggest obstacle to overcome. What you look at and where you allow your mind to wander can be dangerous. You can stir homosexual lust simply by people watching; meditating on past sexual experiences; thinking about pictures, gifts, or belongings from past partners; watching sex scenes in movies; or interacting closely with homosexuals. You must be aware of your surroundings and be conscious of your thoughts. You have to take authority over your mind and your flesh and walk through the deliverance process. You must be delivered. Remember that one look, left unchecked, led to David's downfall.

UNRESOLVED ANGER

Moses had an issue of anger. When the children of Israel became thirsty, they complained against Moses and Aaron.

> And there was no water for the congregation: and they gathered themselves together against Moses and against Aaron. And the people chode with Moses, and spake, saying, Would God that we had died when our brethren died before the Lord! And why have ye brought up the congregation of the Lord into this wilderness, that we and our cattle should die there? . . .
> Take the rod, and gather thou the assembly together, thou and Aaron thy brother, and speak ye unto the rock before their eyes; and it shall give forth his water, and thou shalt bring forth to them water out of the rock: so thou shalt give the congregation and their beasts drink.
> And Moses took the rod from before the Lord, as he commanded him. And Moses and Aaron gathered the congregation together before the rock, and he said unto them, Hear now, ye rebels; must we fetch ye water out of this rock? And Moses lifted up his hand and smote the rock twice: and the water came out abundantly, and the congregation drank, and their beasts also. (Num. 20:2–4, 8–11)

Because Moses had some unresolved anger, it eventually caught up with him. This issue caused him to disobey the Lord's command, which was to *speak* to the rock, not strike it. God wanted the glory. Because Moses hit the rock twice, this looked as if his own strength brought water out of the rock. This incident resulted in Moses not being allowed to enter the Promised Land.

> And the Lord spake unto Moses and Aaron, Because ye believed me not, to sanctify me in the eyes of the children of Israel, therefore ye shall not bring this congregation into the land which I have given them. (Num. 20:12)

If you search the Scriptures, you will see that Moses continually dealt with his anger. Let's start back in Egypt before he knew the Lord. That's where he murdered another man (See Exod. 2:12). Later, after spending forty days and nights on Mount Sinai with God, he got so angry with the children of Israel that he broke the tablets that had the Ten Commandments inscribed on them by the finger of God (See Exod. 32:15–19). Verse 19 says, "Moses' anger waxed hot." This problem followed Moses throughout his life and eventually caused him to miss the blessedness of the Promised Land.

Many who are caught up in the homosexual lifestyle have unresolved anger. They are angry because of the babysitter who molested them. They are angry because of the uncle who abused them. They are angry because of the parent who abandoned them. They refuse to release this anger. Even after receiving Christ, they struggle with anger and bitterness. This issue needs to be dealt with.

An issue left unprocessed in our life eventually causes us to miss God in some way. We will not enjoy the fullness of the benefits of the kingdom of God in this present life. It's not that we won't enter heaven. But we may miss the fullness of the kingdom of God right here and now. God wants us to enjoy all the benefits of salvation while here on this earth. Our relationship to God is more than just going to heaven.

SELF-RIGHTEOUSNESS

The rich young ruler also had an issue. (See Luke 18:18–23) He came to Jesus and asked what he needed to do to inherit eternal life. When Jesus mentioned some of the Ten Commandments, the rich young ruler claimed that he had kept all of those since he was a youth. Jesus told him that he was lacking one thing and told him to sell all that he had, distribute it to the poor, and to follow Him. The rich young ruler walked away from Jesus sorrowful.

This young man's issue was self-righteousness. This is a problem in our churches today. How many homosexuals in the church have been held in such high esteem that they are convinced of their righteousness? Churches have failed to deal with homosexuals who lead the choir. Churches have failed to deal with homosexuals on the deacon board. Churches have failed to deal with homosexual musicians. Not only have churches turned a blind eye to this issue, but they have esteemed these people so highly that they are convinced that they too are the righteousness of God. What a grave mistake to ignore their sin. This needs to be dealt with so that those in bondage can come to know truth and deliverance.

The apostle Paul had an issue. The following passages echo the cry of his heart regarding this subject.

Ye know how through the *infirmity of the flesh* I preached the gospel unto you at the first. And *my temptation which was in my flesh* ye despised not, nor rejected; but received me as an angel of God, even as Christ Jesus. (Gal. 4:13–14)

For I know that in me (that is in my flesh,) dwelleth no good thing: for to will is present with me; but how to perform that which is good I find not. For the good that I would, I do not: but the evil which I would not, that I do. Now if I do that I would not, it is no more I that do it but sin that dwelleth in me. I find then a law, that, when I would do good, evil is present with me. For I delight in the law of God after the inward man: But I see another law in my members, warring against the law of my mind, and *bringing me into captivity* to the law of sin which is in my members. O wretched man that I am! Who can *deliver* me from the body of this death? I thank God through Jesus Christ our Lord. So then with the mind I myself serve the law of God; but with the flesh the law of sin. (Rom. 7:18–25)

What was Paul trying to say? Sometimes our flesh rises up so much that we allow ourselves to become subject to it. We do things that we don't want to do; the things that we want to do, we don't do. A war rages inside of us. We have some issues. The apostle Paul knew that if anyone can deliver us, it is Jesus Christ. He also had the revelation of our position in Christ: "There is therefore now no condemnation to them which are in Christ Jesus, who walk not after the flesh, but after the Spirit" (Rom. 8:1).

Even the mightiest men of God were imperfect. Therefore we cannot allow ourselves to fall into condemnation. These examples aren't a cop-out for not allowing the Lord to process our issues, however. Their lives should encourage us to live fully before God. Yes, they were mighty men of God. Yes, they led thousands. Yes, they had some struggles. But the Bible also shows us what happens when issues are left unprocessed—even in the lives of mighty men of God.

Our heart cry should be, "Lord, no matter what it takes, I want You to process me. I will not walk in condemnation, but I will go through this process. I know that if I allow You to do Your work inside me, I will come out as pure gold."

9. No Condemnation

The apostle Paul knew that no good thing dwelt in his flesh. But he also understood the benefit of being found in Christ. "There is therefore now no condemnation to them which are in Christ Jesus, who walk not after the flesh, but after the Spirit" (Rom. 8:1).

Webster's Dictionary defines "*condemn*" as: 1. *To declare to be reprehensible, wrong, or evil usually without weighing evidence and without reservation*; 2a. *To pronounce guilty, convict;* b. *sentence, doom*; 3. *To adjudge unfit for use or consumption.*

Wow! Doesn't that give you some insight into the purpose of condemnation?

THE BATTLE IN YOUR MIND

Condemnation is one of the biggest tools that the enemy uses against Christians. He loves for you to feel guilty and full of shame. He wants you to feel like you deserve to be punished. He wants you to think that you are evil and unfit to be used by God. He knows that if he can get you feeling badly enough about yourself, he can use that as a foothold to have you abandon the process that God is trying to take you through. The enemy loves to blame and accuse you. This is why the Word of God describes him as being "the accuser of the brethren" (Rev. 12:10).

Many times throughout my Christian walk, and especially through this deliverance process, the enemy has tried to gain a foothold through condemnation. He accused me in my mind over the issues that I faced in my flesh and my spirit. He told me that people really didn't believe I was no longer a lesbian. He had me believe that people looked at me and judged me in their minds. "They smile at you, but they call you a lesbian behind your back."

he whispered. He tried to convince me that if I was really saved, I would not still be dealing with this issue.

The real battle begins in your mind. You must know without a doubt that you are saved and have been washed in the blood of Jesus. You must get Romans 8:1 in your spirit. You have to be absolutely positive that the Lord loves you and that He is on your side. You have to stand firm against the wiles of the devil. You have to keep him in his rightful place—under your feet (See Rom. 16:20). Do not allow him to gain a foothold in your mind through condemnation.

You have to know that it was the Lord's will to reveal your issue to you. God did it for the purpose of purifying you. God is not trying to kill you in the process. He desires to refine and deliver you because He wants to use you. If you have submitted to the process, you are exactly where God wants you. Because the devil is a liar, he will lie and trick you into believing that God is upset with you and you should be upset with yourself.

Do not submit to the lies of the devil. You have to know that you are of great worth to God. You are His child, and He loves you with an everlasting love. Right now. Right where you are. Just as you are—even in the midst of your issues. But now He's calling you up a little higher. It is time for purpose to be exacted in your life.

ARMED WITH SCRIPTURE

When the enemy tries to condemn you, you must be armed with the Word of God. You need verses that will confirm who you are in Christ. For example, "Therefore, if any man be in Christ, he is a new creature: old things are past away; behold all things are become new" (2 Cor. 5:17). You need scriptures that confirm who God is to you. "The Lord is my rock, and my fortress, and my deliverer; my God, my strength, in whom I will trust; my buckler and the horn of my salvation, and my high tower" (Ps. 18:2). You also need a portion of Scripture that is packed with revelation about who God is to us and who we are to God.

> What shall we say then to these things? If God be for us, who can be against us? He that spared not his own Son, but delivered him up for us all, how shall he not with him also freely give us all things? Who shall lay anything to the charge of God's elect? It is God that justifieth. Who is he that condemneth? It is Christ that died, yea rather, that is risen again, who is even at the right hand of God, who also maketh intercession for us. Who shall separate us from the love of Christ? Shall tribulation, or distress, or persecution, or famine, or nakedness, or peril, or sword? As it is written, For thy sake we are killed all the day long; we are accounted as sheep for the slaughter. Nay, in all these things we are more than conquerors through him that loved us. For I am persuaded, that neither death, nor life, nor angels, nor principalities, nor power, nor things present, nor things to come, nor height, nor depth, nor any other creature, shall be able to separate us from the love of God, which is in Christ Jesus our Lord. (Rom. 8:31–39)

Hallelujah! That passage does something inside me. I recommend selecting some appropriate Bible verses, writing them out with a big marker, and posting them in your bedroom or throughout your house. When I was in process, I had scriptures in my room, on my fridge, on posters in my living room, and on the mirror in my bathroom. If you do not want to post anything in your home or you don't have your own space, then write these verses on a piece of paper and review them frequently so that they are in your heart.

When you need these truths, the Holy Ghost can bring them back to your remembrance. "But the Comforter, which is the Holy Ghost, whom the Father will send in my name, he shall teach you all things, and bring all things to your remembrance, whatsoever I have said unto you" (John 14:26). These scriptures will be extremely helpful to you whenever condemnation comes your way.

READY FOR THE CHALLENGE?

Condemnation comes in many different shapes and forms. The enemy can even use people to bring condemnation. People may challenge you and where you are in your walk with the Lord. People may question whether or not you have truly been delivered. Some may challenge you verbally; others may try to undermine you with a mere facial expression. Some pretend that they are really concerned about you, but really they just want to get in your business to see if you are really delivered.

When these people come, do not subject yourself to condemnation. It doesn't matter at what stage you find yourself. You may be completely delivered, having gone through the process. You may be delivered in the sense that you are saved and have been transitioned into a place of safety and no longer participate in unclean acts. If you come under attack, you should rejoice. If the enemy challenges you, that means you're on the right track. He gets nervous when it comes to deliverance. He desperately wants to hold you in bondage. If he cannot hold you in bondage to the issue itself, then he tries to hold you in bondage to condemnation.

After I had come out of my process, I was challenged publicly while visiting a church. A woman, who sat in the pew in front of me, turned around and engaged me in conversation during the service.

"Are you that girl who used to be a lesbian?" she loudly asked.

"Yes, ma'am," I said.

"Are you really delivered?"

"Yes, ma'am, I am," I declared.

"Are you sure you are delivered?" she asked in a challenging tone of voice.

"Yes, ma'am, I am sure."

"Cause if you're not," she said, "I'll call you out right here!"

I just smiled and calmly assured her that I was delivered. The entire time that the enemy was challenging me through this lady, I remained calm, peaceful, and at ease.

I had two friends with me that evening, one sitting on each side of me. Both of them heard the entire conversation. So did others seated around us because of her loud tone of voice. The next day, one of my friends said, "Autumn, I don't know how you stayed so calm with that lady last night. I would have gone off!"

PASSING THE TEST

To be honest, I was a little surprised myself on how calmly I reacted. In the past, I would have been absolutely humiliated by her lack of tact. But now that I was truly delivered, I didn't have anything to prove to this sister. The grace of God stepped in so that I could be an example in that situation.

On the evening of the incident, my other friend who was with me told me that the lady who challenged me had struggled with lesbianism for years. I believe she had heard me testify about being delivered from the lesbian lifestyle in her church before. When I found out about her struggle, I realized why she would challenge me like she did. Because she may have still been struggling, it was hard for her to believe that I could be delivered. Not only that, but the enemy tests us every once in a while to see if he can provoke us, disgrace us, or condemn us. This was just a test. But I am happy to say that by the grace of God, I passed that test. Since the incident, I have earnestly prayed for this sister to be delivered.

However condemnation tries to come at you, do not allow it to gain a foothold in your life. A life free of condemnation promotes spiritual growth. Whatever the issues in your life may be, just go through the process. Continue to remind yourself who you are in the Lord.

Speak into your own life. Don't wait for a prophet. The words of life are in your mouth. Sometimes we have to be like David and encourage ourselves in the Lord. Look into the mirror and prophesy over your own life. Preach to yourself.

You must have a by-any-means-necessary mentality. You need a mindset that says, "I don't care what the devil tries to whisper in my ear. I am who God says I am. I will do what God says I will do. I will be who God says I will be. I will never give up. It may cost me everything, but I will never give up. I am going forward and not backward. I am not a backslider. I am saved, and I will press in for my complete deliverance in the name of Jesus."

10. ALONE WITH GOD: SANCTIFICATION AND SEPARATION

A few days after returning home from the conference where I went to the alter and began my process of deliverance from homosexuality, the Lord woke me up at 5:30 a.m. and began to minister to me. Here is an excerpt from my journal from that morning:

Thank You, Jesus. Thank You that I am about to undergo surgery. You are going to cut out those things that hinder me from getting to the other side. To my wealthy place. To the Promised Land. Into the fullness of Your purpose and plan for my life. Into deeper, more intimate relationship. Lord, I thank You for the old that will be purged and the new wine that will be poured in. Thank You, Jesus, for the squeeze because out of it comes the best. Have Your way, Lord. Speak to my heart. I love You. Your servant, Autumn.

I certainly had an expectation in my heart. I didn't know exactly how God would do it, but I knew it would be for my ultimate good.

LIVING ALONE

The Lord was ready to purge me and take me through a process. Little did I know that this process would require solitary times with God. Jesus set this example of stealing away to be alone with His Father. "And in the morning, rising up a great while before day, he went out; and departed into a solitary place; and there prayed" (Mark 1:35).

Within three weeks of coming home from the conference a new opportunity arose for me. I had been living with my parents for a while and really wanted a place of my own. My pastor's aunt had been staying in a one bedroom house near my church in San Diego, and my pastor informed me that she was ready to move out. My pastor suggested that I move in. Ecstatic about the opportunity, I began making the arrangements and moved in the following month. Shortly after that I received a promotion on my job, and things looked good for me.

I had to adjust to living by myself. I had never lived alone before and didn't know what to expect. For so many years I had felt the need to surround myself with people. This season was quite the opposite of that. It felt good to have a place to call my own. I enjoyed the peace and quiet. Most of all, I began to enjoy the benefits of unhindered prayer. I could be as free as I wanted in my time with the Lord. I did not need to hold back because others were in the house within earshot. I was as free as I could be in the presence of my Father.

A PLACE OF PURGING

Throughout the next few months I began to experience some warfare in my mind. Lustful thoughts, thoughts of past experiences, and memories from sexual activities plagued me. I refused to subject myself to these thoughts and continued to cast down imaginations. I got in God's Word and began to study the mind. I focused on the apostle Paul's exhortation to "be renewed in the spirit of your mind" (Eph. 4:23). I found out that the word *renewed* in the Greek means: *to renovate*; i.e. *to reform*. Some renovating and reforming definitely needed to happen in my mind.

I began to study Jesus and His wilderness experience (See Luke 4:1–13). Immediately after He was filled with the Holy Ghost, He was led into the wilderness. Because He had fasted and denied Himself, He overcame the temptations of the devil. I looked at how Jesus used the Word of God to confront temptation. Then I realized that the Spirit led Jesus into the wilderness to be tempted of the devil.

We go through things for a reason and a purpose. I realized that if God puts you in the wilderness, it is for a purpose. When He accomplishes that purpose, He will bring you out. During times of temptation, I needed not to give up but to defeat the enemy with the Word of God. These things happened to me to glorify God and to bring me closer to Him. God did not intend to kill me but to strengthen and teach me.

I began to see that this wilderness was for the purpose of process. God wanted to purify some things in my life. The wilderness is a necessary place—a place of purging and refining. I needed not to complain about the process in the wilderness, for this would only take my eyes off Jesus and extend my stay. I needed to rejoice and give God praise in the middle of the wilderness so that I could journey through.

Needless to say, the battles in my mind intensified. I wondered what was going on. I battled confusion and had difficulty understanding why these thoughts plagued my mind. I continued to study the Word of God and pray, but the Lord wanted something more from me.

A WORD FROM GOD

One night the Lord spoke to me while in prayer. Here is an excerpt from my journal:

I have called you and ordained you from before the foundation of the world. There are some things I need to tell you. Things I need to impart into your spirit. But you have to have a consistent place of stillness and quietness—a solitary place. I need you to hear Me. All distracting noises and voices must be blocked out. I am going to speak in My still small voice, but you shall be able to hear Me, if you have this secret place. For you shall know My voice. The directions I give, you must obey and carry out. You must do as I say. Don't worry about anything. I am in control. I will be in your mouth. It is not you who will speak, but it is I who will speak through you. But you must open your mouth with boldness. Be not afraid for I am with thee. I will lead thee. All of your needs will be taken care of. Nations shall call you blessed. But you must lay down your life and follow Me. Remember that you are a holy thing, a consecrated and dedicated thing. Holiness. "Be thou holy for I the Lord thy God am holy." Take no thought for tomorrow. I hear your prayers, your petitions and requests, your intercessions and concerns. Know that it's all taken care of, for I am the Lord thy God. I not only hear but I answer. Just stay focused on Me. Stay focused on Me.

Three days later while in a prayer meeting at my church, a sister prophetically spoke into my life. "God has made you a warrior," she declared. "He has placed you on the front line of the battle. God is teaching you how to do battle. He is giving you strategy to defeat the enemy."

Three days after that my pastor met me outside of the church after the service. She began to speak into my life, saying that the Lord will begin to call me into a place of solitude, a place of intimacy—one on one with the Lord. He will establish deep, intimate relationship between us. She said that I had to have this place to prepare me for the calling, the ministry. "This is a place that will call you away from people. There will be a sanctification and a separation. This will be a lonely place, but it is to build relationship with the Lord, and it is necessary for the calling."

Three days later my other pastor came to me and said that God was calling me to a place of separation. "Separation from people and things," he declared. "He is going to begin to call you away from people and unto Himself. This is to establish deep, intimate relationship with God. He has called you unto Himself for a purpose. You must throw up your hands and say yes. It is only for a season, but it must happen. You will not be lonely, but you will be alone with God."

Now if I didn't get the message after all of that, I deserved to live in the wilderness for the rest of my life. Obviously God was calling me to Himself. The Lord desired to do some things in my life, but it would require intimacy. Time alone with God.

A PLACE OF INTIMACY

Intimacy is more than just reading the Bible, praying, and attending church. Intimacy requires the investment of time, space, and energy. Intimacy requires communication. Not one-sided communication, but listening as well as speaking. Intimacy is a place where things are revealed in secret. It is a place exclusively between two parties. It is a place where intimate experiences occur; no words can give it justice.

Intimacy is a revealing place for both parties involved. It always involves exposure of the two. In-to-me-see, this is intimacy. See-in-to-me, this is intimacy. It's you asking God to see into you, and as a result you get to see into God. It's a place of humility and submission. A place of surrender. A place where you are completely naked and exposed before your Maker. A place where every mask is taken off and the truth about you is revealed. This is the place of intimacy. It is the place where relationship is built. It is more than an act or ritual; it is relationship. It is love-making. It is more to be desired than anything else.

This place of intimacy cannot take place with others around. It requires alone time with the Lord. Many people do not submit themselves to this place with God and as a result do not enjoy the benefits of really walking with Him. In this place the Lord begins to show you the inner recesses of your heart. He exposes the issues of your life that need to be exposed. You may go into this place with issues that you are aware of, like I did. The issue of homosexuality was obviously still there. But that was at the surface of many other issues that needed to be exposed in order for my healing to occur. As I entered into intimacy with the Lord, I began to see deeper into my heart.

My friend, you are going to have to spend some time alone with God if you plan on being delivered from the issues of your life. In the beginning, it may seem like you are wasting your time. It may seem like nothing is happening. But I dare you to just stay there. Stay in a secret place with God. Make a commitment to spend time on your face before the Lord. Set the atmosphere. Dim the lights. It's time to get intimate with the Lover of your soul. Tell Him about Himself. Let Him hear you tell Him how wonderful He is to you. Tell Him about His beauty, His splendor, His majesty. Share with Him the way He makes you feel inside. Let worship flow from your innermost being. Let your face hit your carpet.

Lay out before Him. Listen for His voice. Open the eyes of your heart, and see what He will speak. Hear His affirmations of who you are in Him. See through the eyes of His holiness those things that are repulsive. Feel the comfort of His presence. Ask Him to help you in the areas in which you need help. Ask Him to burn out everything not like Him. Allow Him to show you the places that are hard to look at. The things that you don't want to remember. The things that you don't want to see. Let the tears flow freely. There is no reservation in this place. There is nowhere to hide but in Him. Rest in the comfort that His love for you is undying and everlasting. My God . . . I'm talking about being alone with God.

We have "prayer" when other people are around. We have "prayer" in church and among other folks. But we have intimacy when we are alone with God. Are you willing to be alone with God? Are you willing to get into a solitary place? A place where no one is around. A place where it's just you and God.

YOUR PRIVATE LIFE

I heard a preacher say, "Your public life is only a secondary result of your private life." You may hear someone pray powerfully in public. It may not necessarily be what they say when they pray, or how eloquently they speak, but the presence of God that you feel when they pray. You wonder what about this person invokes such a powerful presence of the Lord in the atmosphere.

That is simply a secondary result of their life of intimacy with the Lord when no one is around. It is that person's life in private that makes him so powerful in public. It is your time alone with God that empowers you to be a life changer in public. If you would just be alone with God, the presence of God will be on your life.

You can talk to your friends all day. You can bring your problems, circumstances, and situations to others all day long. You can cry to others about what's going on inside of you. Don't get me wrong. I believe in speaking to others about what's going on in your life and having people pray for you. I believe in the prayer of agreement. I believe that in times of warfare, you need people with the power to rebuke the enemy from your life. But if you do all that and don't spend *any* time alone with God yourself, you're probably not going to come out with the intimacy that God intended you to have.

Relationship is built through experiences. It requires good times, fun times, as well as hard times and trying times. Some of my greatest relationships were born out of adversity. How do you know if you have relationships? Look at the people who are there when times are rough. Their presence in adversity proves you have relationship. If you want to be around me only when everything is going great, then we are just acquaintances. Do you want to be there when I don't feel like smiling and joking around? Can you hang in there when all hell is breaking loose in my life? Will you stay when the tears are flowing? If you can be there for me through all these things, and still love me the same way, then you are my friend.

It is the same with the Lord. Do we come to Him only when we're full of joy? Do we pray only when things are going our way? Then we are just acquaintances. God is just someone I kick it with when life is great. If the fires of afflictions hit my life, and I run to everyone else but never run to God, then we don't have relationship. We do not have intimacy. Jesus wants to be involved in every area of our lives, but we would rather be comforted by others than by the Ruler of the universe. He holds your answer. He doesn't want to be your acquaintance. He wants to be your everything.

The Lord wants to be alone with you. For the process of deliverance to take place, for relationship with Jesus Christ to be built, and for preparation for the calling upon your life, being alone with God is absolutely necessary. It is a beautiful thing. I dare you to try it, if you haven't already. Your life will be changed forever. Nothing can compare to the beauty of intimacy with the Lord Jesus Christ.

It's more than the presence of the Lord on Sunday during a church service. It is the presence of God in your home, on your job, in your car, at the grocery store. It is Emmanuel, God with us. It is sharing yourself with God wholly and completely. Let's face it. God knows everything about us. Nothing is hid from Him. But He wants you to benefit from relationship with Him. He wants to reveal Himself to you in ways that will only happen in alone time with God.

If we just got saved, kept on living, and never went through rough times, then we would never grow in our relationship with the Lord. Does God have the power to deliver you out of every issue of your life in an instant? Of course He does. He is All Powerful. Then why did I have to go through all that happened in my childhood? Why is it that, even as a Christian, issues still follow me? Why do I face situations where it doesn't even look like God is anywhere to be found?

I struggled with some of these questions myself. But from personal experience, I found out that God wanted an intimate relationship with me. Only through an intimate relationship with God would I fulfill the calling that He has placed on my life. It would take intimacy for me to be a true witness of the delivering power of God. In the alone times, the times of intimacy, I would see myself as He sees me. In these times I would see Him in ways that I had never seen Him before. Deliverance would come to me in these intimate moments.

GOD HAS A PURPOSE

The Lord does not allow us to go through trying times for no reason at all. No. He always has a purpose. He is all knowing. If He just snapped His fingers and made our lives so that we never had to go through anything, we would not appreciate our relationship with Him. He knows that we would take Him for granted. We would not have relationship. We would have a spiritual genie who at the snap of a finger delivered us from everything in an instant. He knows we would not have spent times on our face before Him. He knows that our times of prayer would be out of ritual rather than out of relationship. He always has desired intimacy in His relationship with His people. When it comes to his relationship with us, God has a by-any-means-necessary mentality. He will do whatever it takes to get you truly hooked up with Him.

This is all out of love. I am so grateful that I can say that I have an intimate relationship with the Lord. When I think of the growth that has occurred in our relationship, I know that everything that I have gone through has brought me to this point with Him. Although I have not arrived and am not perfect, the beauty of my relationship with Him means more to me than anything. Today I appreciate the Lord. I am ever so grateful to have relationship with Jesus Christ. Many things and many people have influenced my relationship with Him for the better, but time alone with Him birthed the intimacy that we now share.

Don't be afraid to get close with God. Just open up your heart and let Him in. He has the most beautiful love that you will ever experience. He holds your deliverance from every issue from your past. He just waits for you to come to Him. He wants you to come and get Him. In the process of getting Him, you will receive your deliverance. Be alone with God. Get intimate with the Lover of your soul. Jesus is calling you to Himself. He wants to do something more inside you. He desires a closer walk with you. He wants to show you things that you have never seen before. Just come. Just come. In Jesus' name.

11. THE WARRIOR SPIRIT

Throughout my process of deliverance, the Holy Spirit often brought this verse to my remembrance: "For every battle of the warrior is with confused noise, and garments rolled in blood; but this shall be with burning and fuel of fire" (Isa. 9:5). This scripture came to have such significant meaning in my life. In the midst of battles, it continues to remind me who I am. I am a warrior. Webster's Dictionary defines *"warrior"* as: *a man engaged or experienced in warfare; a person engaged in some struggle or conflict.*

FIGHT FOR YOUR LIFE

As I spent time alone with God, it seemed as if the battles in my mind and the struggles in my flesh intensified. I found myself in a place of conflict and confusion. I did not understand what was going on. Now I know that the Lord had begun to teach me how to do battle. He gave me strategies on how to defeat the enemy. These strategies enabled me to rebuke him not only from my life but also from the lives of others.

A battle raged in my life. As the Lord dealt with me about my issues, the enemy intensified and amplified his tactics. As I moved forward, the war continued. My mind became the battleground. The majority of our battles are fought right here. When we allow the Lord to process us, the enemy fights us on every front. He does everything he can to make you give up in the middle of the process. He loves nothing more than to see you throw in the towel and curse God. As my desire to allow the Lord to process me intensified, so did the warfare in my mind.

Many times the thoughts in my mind brought confusion. They often sounded like a bunch of noise—just clutter and confusion.

Have you ever seen a cartoon character that has an angel on one shoulder and the devil on the other shoulder? Both voices speak into an ear, trying to turn the will of the cartoon character. This is a loud place, a place that is not easy to understand. This is spiritual warfare. The enemy launches many attacks in the mind.

In these times a believer must continue to press into God. This is where you have to begin to fight. This is where you show what you are made of. This is where the warrior spirit is birthed. You will either do one of two things: fight for your life or lie down and die. I chose to fight for my life.

Jesus had to fight against the devil in the wilderness, and so do we. Jesus was led by the Spirit into the wilderness (Luke 4:1), just as we are led by the Spirit into the wilderness of process. This occurs for the purpose of God to be fulfilled. Although the Holy Spirit led Jesus into this place, Jesus still had to fight to overcome those temptations. The Father wanted to prepare Him for the mission of proclaiming God's kingdom.

We go through many things in the process. It may feel like a wilderness, dry times, and a lonely or solitary place. But the Spirit often leads us into this place for a purpose. God has a plan for our lives. Although we do not have the blueprint for that plan, God does. He knows our beginning, our end, and all that we will go through in the process. But if the Spirit leads you in, you have to believe that the Spirit will lead you out. But we have to learn how to fight.

When we go through the process, this brings glory to God. These places bring us closer to Him. They establish intimate relationship. They teach us to trust in Him. They teach us how to be skilled warriors. They teach us how to fight. If God takes you through this process, it is not to kill you. It is to strengthen you, to purify you, to prepare you, to make you ready for the next place, and to teach you how to do warfare.

SUBMIT AND RESIST

The enemy has only as much power as the Lord allows him to have. He can go only as far as the Lord allows him to go. I heard a preacher say that "the enemy has a big bark, but God holds the leash." We have to submit ourselves to God and fight the enemy. "Submit yourselves therefore to God. Resist the devil, and he will flee from you" (James 4:7).

The first part of this battle tactic is to submit to God. You have to submit to God calling you to time alone with Him. He wants to deal with some issues in your life. Are you ready for that? Do you realize that your relationship with the Lord may cost you everything? The Lord called you for a reason that goes far beyond your own salvation. He wants to use you for His glory that others may be born into His kingdom.

Are you willing to submit to the call? If you are not willing, there's no point in moving on to the next portion of this verse. The enemy already has you where he wants you. If you are unwilling to submit, there's no battle. He just waits for the right time to come in and devour you. But if you submit yourself to God, you will face some warfare. After submission comes resistance.

At this point in my life, my mind was made up. I was going to go forth in the name of the Lord. I did not come this far to allow the enemy to take me out. I was willing to fight for my life. I allowed Him to take me through the deliverance process. I hated everything that I saw within me that was not like God. I was not in agreement with the issues of homosexuality. I wanted every piece of residue from that lifestyle to be burned out of my life. A violence rose up within me when I realized that an enemy was trying to take me out. This violence is necessary. This is the violence of the warrior spirit. "And from the days of John the Baptist until now the kingdom of heaven suffereth violence, and the violent take it by force" (Matt. 11:12).

When the Bible instructs us to "resist the devil" (James 4:7), it does not mean to run away, avoid conflict, or be scared of the devil. We can't back away from the fight. Webster's Dictionary defines *"resist"* as: *vigorously opposing; to withstand; fend off; to oppose actively; to fight against.* After we submit to God, we have to position ourselves to violently oppose the devil. We have the power to go against him. As soon as we submit to God, the fight begins. Now we have been given the authority to fend off the enemy and finish it. We *will* fight against him and we *will* prevail.

We are not to back away from the devil, but he is supposed to back away from us. We are supposed to fight—not give up or give in, but fight. My pastor gave me the best counsel that I ever received. It was one sentence. "*You* need to put *your* face to the wall, pray, and rebuke the devil." Simple but yet so profound. In other words, *you* pray. *You* seek God. *You* fight the devil. *You* do warfare in your home. *You* war in the spiritual realm. There are some wars that *you* need to learn how to fight.

Jesus said, "Behold, I have given *you* power to tread on serpents and scorpions, and over all the power of the enemy; and nothing shall by any means hurt you" (Luke 10:19). He let us know that we have been given the power to defeat the enemy. He has given it to us. We are not supposed to be defeated. If we are defeated, it's because we didn't do something right. We have the power to cause the devil to retreat. We have the same power that Jesus had to fight the enemy in the wilderness. We have the same Scriptures that He used to fend him off.

EQUIPPED FOR WARFARE

The Word of God inside us is our sword (Eph. 6:17), our skilled weapon in defeating the enemy. It is our offense and defense in this battle. We have to keep our sword sharpened. We cannot cut the enemy with a dull sword. We have to get into the Word of God for ourselves. We are going to need the Word to fight. It has to be in us. Sometimes battles come quickly. If you are not prepared, you will be caught off guard. You won't always have time to look for your Bible and find a verse. The Word of God has to be in you. If it is in you, then it will come out of you when you need it.

We have to go into warfare equipped. We have to wear our armor. God has provided a piece to protect every part of us.

> Put on the whole armor of God, that ye may be able to stand against the wiles of the devil. For we wrestle not against flesh and blood, but against principalities and powers, against the rulers of the darkness of this world, against spiritual wickedness in high places. Wherefore, take unto you the whole armor of God, that ye may be able to withstand in the evil day, and having done all, to stand. Stand therefore, having your loins girt about with truth, and having on the breastplate of righteousness; and your feet shod with the preparation of the gospel of peace; Above all, taking the shield of faith, wherewith ye shall be able to quench all the fiery darts of the wicked. And take the helmet of salvation, and the sword of the Spirit, which is the word of God: Praying always with all prayer and supplication in the Spirit, and watching thereunto with all perseverance and supplication for all saints. (Eph. 6:11–18)

How can we be equipped for battle? Just look at those verses. We need the full armor of God. We have to put it on. As we "put off" all the stuff that is not like God, we must "put on" the whole armor of God. As we "put off," the enemy will come. But if we have "put on" the whole armor of God, we will be equipped to fight off the enemy.

BATTLING CONFUSION

Remember my verse for warfare? "For every battle of the warrior is with confused noise, and garments rolled in blood; but this shall be with burning and fuel of fire" (Isa. 9:6).

When you get serious about your deliverance, you may experience times of confusion. The warfare in your mind may intensify. It is rising because that issue is ready to come out of you. It has been revealed and is coming to the surface so that it can be dealt with and assassinated. Death is near for that issue, and the enemy knows it.

Here is an excerpt from my journal in my time of confusion during my struggle with the residue of homosexuality:

Lord, deliver me from the confusion in my mind. I desire to love with the purity of Your love. Show me how to love with pureness of heart. Let all evil be far removed from me. Let Your Spirit be in control. Let the flesh be crucified. The Spirit is willing, but the flesh is weak. Deliver my mind. Oh, Lord Jesus, I want to put on Your mind. The enemy cannot have my mind in the name of Jesus. I plead the blood of Jesus.

I need You to teach me how to love. Let me love with no twists, no perversion, no lust . . . just pure love. When Jonathan loved David as his own soul, that's deep love but yet still pure, right? I'm scared because I don't want my love to turn into lust. It makes it difficult to truly give my heart to others. I want to, but I don't trust myself because I can feel the flesh trying to get into everything and twist it.

Lord, help me. Make me whole. I don't want to sin against You. Not in my thoughts, my motives, or outwardly in any way. God, I feel like this thing has come about so suddenly and un-expectantly. I mean on and off it's been there. But now all of a sudden I feel weak in my flesh. Not having control of my thoughts. What's going on, Lord? Isaiah 9:6. This is what You were warning me about way back then, huh?

> *Well, Lord, I need Your help. Here I am. I yield and surrender to thee. Purify my heart. Purge my thoughts. Make me clean. Forgive me, Jesus. Wash me in Your blood. I need Thee, O Lord. Have mercy, Thou Son of David. Have mercy. I am your daughter. You are my Father. And I do love You above all.*
> *Autumn*

This excerpt is so sloppy, and I remember crying as I wrote it. The handwriting reminds me of my struggle. It shows the intensity that I felt as I penned my heart's cry to the Lord. The confusion almost overwhelmed me. But as you can see, I continued to run to my Father. I poured out my heart to Him. I trusted Him enough to share the deepest, darkest emotions of my soul. He knew all about it anyway.

As time passed, I continued to fight. I recall many times walking through my house, praying in the spirit, speaking in tongues, commanding the enemy, opening my door and telling him, "Get out!" I spent many hours on the carpet of my home, crying out to the Lord to deliver me. I anointed myself and my home with oil. My neighbors probably thought that I had lost my mind. I'm sure they heard me during times of serious warfare. Much prayer, much fighting, much worship, much praise, much Scripture, much crying, much fasting. I had a by-any-means-necessary mentality. The Lord had worked a warrior spirit in me. I hated the enemy and the issue of homosexuality that was trying to take me out.

FUEL FOR THE FIRE

Little did I know that this time of warfare, this time of confusion, would be just what Isaiah 9:6 said for me: "burning and fuel of fire." This confusion and warfare set me on fire by the Holy Ghost. This warfare propelled me into another level with the Lord. Much power will come out of this place of confusion. Just continue to fight and to press. You will come out a skilled warrior. You will come out with power and with an anointing that will be evident.

During this time, the anointing would be so strong on me that I sometimes ended up on the floor of the church. I began having dreams, visions, and prophetic insight. I can't share these experiences with everybody because some may think I have lost my mind. But when you really begin to walk in the spirit, God reveals things to you that are completely spiritual. The natural, carnal mind cannot understand these things. My pastor once told me that there is a fine line between the spiritual world and the natural world. Some experiences that you may have will be a temporary crossing over. It's nothing new. It happened to men in the Bible. And it is happening all over the world today, in the lives of men and women of God who are willing to crucify the flesh and seek the Lord.

Just press in, my friend. Press past the confusion. Press past the struggles in your flesh. Allow the warrior spirit to rise up within you, and fight the enemy who tries to take your life. Take your battle stance. Get on your knees, lay prostrate, position yourself. God is getting you ready.

When you come out, you are going to be pure gold. When you come out, you will be refined for His glory. You will be elevated in the Spirit. Your relationship will be intimate. Your issue will be purged. You will be purified from that thing that tries to hold you captive. You will be delivered. The yoke will be broken from your life. You will be a "vessel unto honour, sanctified, and meet for the master's use, and prepared unto every good work" (2 Tim. 2:21).

12. GETTING TO THE ROOT

Fallow ground is left uncultivated. It is land that the farmer has not touched for a season. A prophet told the Israelites what to do with their fallow ground. "Sow to yourselves in righteousness, reap in mercy; break up your fallow ground: for it is time to seek the Lord, till he come and rain righteousness upon you" (Hosea 10:12).

What does fallow ground mean for us? These are the hidden areas of our lives that are hard to reach. Those painful experiences. Those shameful memories. The hurtful things. Those experiences that helped to shape who you are. That uncultivated land needs to be broken up. That soil needs to be tilled. That ground needs to be exposed to the Holy Spirit so that it can be tilled and new seeds—seeds of righteousness—can be planted.

I want to reiterate that I take full responsibility for living the lesbian lifestyle. I take full responsibility for all my actions and other damnable things that I have done. Nobody ever forced me into doing the things that I did. My actions were my choice and I own up to them. I allowed myself to get involved in the lesbian lifestyle. My past did not *make* me do it, but I *chose* to do it. I want to make that clear before we move forward.

UPROOTING SIN'S DOMINION

I am not going to expound on the obvious, which is that we are all "shapen in iniquity" and conceived in sin (Ps. 51:5) as a result of the fall of man. Our sinful nature is definitely at the root of the issues that mankind faces. Had there never been sin in the beginning, man never would have been separated from God. None of us would have a sinful nature.

This is the seed that must first be uprooted in our lives. That's why Jesus said, "Ye must be born again" (John 3:7). The seed of sin's dominion must be uprooted and the incorruptible seed of the Word of God must be planted. "Being born again, not of corruptible seed, but of incorruptible, by the word of God, which liveth and abideth forever" (1 Pet. 2:23). Even after we receive this incorruptible seed, issues from our past follow us. Let's look at how to get to the roots of those issues.

Many of us have been through traumatizing experiences. Events and periods of our lives have left us broken and wounded. Some of these experiences have played a vital role in molding and shaping our attitudes, dispositions, character, and ways. These things are real. Many of our issues were birthed out of these experiences. I am not saying that we hold no responsibility for our actions. I believe that a person is fully responsible for his actions and choices. I also believe that events and experiences can strongly affect your life, however. Deeply rooted issues can affect you for years. Your actions are yours. Nobody else is responsible for your actions. But the actions are just an end result of something deeper. There is something at your root.

I have worked with teenagers for years. I know teens that have been through some serious, traumatic experiences. The Lord has placed a burden on my heart for teenagers. I hate to see them struggling. I hate to see them going through the confusion that I went through. I hate to see them longing for parental guidance that their parents are not there to give them. I hate to see them searching for love in all the wrong places. Many are trapped in the same sexual issues that I had. My heart bleeds for them. I have prayed many prayers and cried many tears for them. I feel their struggle.

Many teens stand out in my mind, but I will use one child in particular for an example. By the time he was eleven years old, this child had been sexually abused by his mother for a large portion of his childhood. His mother often had him perform oral sex on her.

By the time I came in contact with this child, it was not hard to see that he was overly sexualized for his age.

One night he had a cleaning supply in his hand during chore time. He sprayed me in the face with the chemical, and another staff member restrained him. He yelled profanities at me, including what he wanted to do to me sexually. This boy was held responsible for his actions because he sprayed me in the face and yelled obscenities at me. It doesn't take a rocket scientist to figure out that this boy had some deep, underlying issues, however. These issues affected him to the point where they had actually shaped his nature. This was not a one-time event. He often made sexual remarks to females.

Had this boy not been sexually abused by his mother, he may not have consistently acted out in such a perverse way at such an early age. This young boy had some underlying issues that had never been dealt with. As a result, he acted them out with perversity. His actions were his responsibility, but he was not responsible for the abuse in his past. I believe that many bad seeds were planted in the life of this young boy. In the same way that good seeds bring forth good fruit, bad seeds take root and bring forth rotten fruit.

GETTING TO THE CORE

In seeking the Lord, spending time alone with God, engaging in warfare, and going through my process of deliverance from homosexuality, I found out that I had some deeply rooted issues. With my background I always knew that I had some issues. As I sought the Lord, however, I saw myself more clearly. The issue of homosexuality was just one of my issues. Beneath that other issues were rooted in the depths of my soul.

The Lord began to show me that it is like an onion. An onion has many layers. Each issue in my life represented a layer. God wanted to strip every layer and get to the core of those issues. He desired to peel off the issues layer by layer. This is the process of deliverance. Earlier I explained that the word delivered comes from the Hebrew word *"chalats"* means: *to pull off; to strip; to depart; to equip for fight* (See Ps. 81:7). This is what deliverance is all about. Stripping to the core. Getting to the root. Going through layers of pain, abuse, torment, blood, tears, hurt, neglect, abandonment, molestation, and anger. Depending on your background, it can go even further.

We cannot stop at salvation if we want to experience true deliverance from our past. Some things need to be dealt with at the root. When you get saved, you may feel the weight of sin lifted from you. The burden of guilt may be gone. Even if you feel the joy of your salvation, some roots may remain. You may not see them at first. If they're below the surface, you'll have to deal with them sooner or later. The Lord says this:

> That I will break the Assyrian in my land, and upon my mountains tread him under foot: than shall his yoke depart from off them, and his burden depart from off their shoulders....
> Rejoice not thou, whole Palestina, because the rod of him that smote thee is broken: for *out of the serpent's root* shall come forth a cockatrice, and his fruit shall be a flying fiery serpent. (Isa. 14:25, 29)

The Lord dealt with the Assyrian, or the enemy, and yokes were destroyed and burdens were lifted from off the people. We get so happy with our salvation, which is definitely something to be excited about. The holy seed has been planted. Some things need to be killed at the root, however. Everything that the enemy has sown needs to be uprooted or your fruit will continue to be maimed and corrupt. Some holy seeds need to be planted in your spirit but especially the incorruptible seed of the Word of God. The ground must be prepared first. These seeds need to be planted so that fresh roots can be formed. Seeds of righteousness form roots of righteousness, which form fruits of righteousness. "For if the firstfruit be holy, the lump is also holy: and if the root be holy, so are the branches" (Rom. 11:16).

LOOK AT YOUR PAST

You must go through this process to truly be delivered. You must allow the Holy Spirit to bring painful experiences back to your remembrance for the purpose of tilling the uncultivated land so that seeds of righteousness can be planted there. The Lord will then send the rain, and righteousness will be the result. *"Righteousness"* is defined as: *the quality of being right; the word suggests conformity to the revealed will of God in all respects.* You will be conformed into the revealed will of God. Wow, that's pretty powerful. Those issues will not hold you bound any longer. Those bad seeds will be tilled, and new seeds will be planted. You will be free and able to move on in the Lord.

Many people like to skip this process. They say that once you are saved, you are a new creation and all the old stuff doesn't need to be dealt with. Just forget those things and move on in your life with Christ. Many of these same people have issues that have never been dealt with. Some are so obvious that everyone can see them. Some Christians are just downright mean. Some Christians have anger that flares up. Many Christians are jealous and envious of others. When these people get in tight situations, their responses often reveal that they have not allowed the Holy Spirit to process those areas.

Deeper issues lie beneath all of that anger, meanness, jealousy, and envy. We see only a glimpse of what is going on inside. The Lord will continue to allow the tight situations to occur so those areas will manifest. He wants you to see and admit that you need to work on some things. These areas need to be cleansed, purged, and uprooted. A process needs to take place in the life of every Christian. It is dangerous to yourself and to others for you not to let the Lord have His way. You can be more of a damaging witness than a beneficial witness. The Lord wants to get good fruit out of your life. Listen to Jesus speak a parable:

> A certain man had a fig tree planted in his vineyard; and he came and sought fruit thereon, and found none. Then said he unto the dresser of his vineyard, Behold, these three years I come seeking fruit on this fig tree, and find none: cut it down; why cumbereth it the ground? And he answering said unto him, Lord let it alone this year also, till I shall dig about it, and dung it: And if it bear fruit, well: and if not, then after that thou shalt cut it down. (Luke 13:6–9)

What a powerful illustration of what the Lord requires. He requires fruit—good fruit—to come forth from you. He will not settle for you just taking up space in the church. The Lord wants more out of you than church attendance. He wants fruit. Let Him dig about you. Let Him dung you. Allow the fruit inspector to have His way.

I am a living witness that these issues need to be processed out by the Spirit of God if you want to get all that God has for you in this life. You have to allow your past to be healed so that you can be propelled forward in power. It is like a slingshot and a rock. God represents the slingshot, and we represent the rock. He places us in the slingshot and pulls us back. The further back the rock is pulled, the more resistance the slingshot feels. It gets harder to pull the slingshot back the farther you pull it. But the farther back the slingshot is pulled, when it is released, the more force the rock will have and the farther the rock will soar. If we allow the Lord to pull us back into our past for the purpose of healing, He will propel us forward with great force and power. He wants to supply us with so much power that any devil that gets in the way will be annihilated.

During this point of the process we must allow the Spirit of God to take us back. We must reflect on past experiences, pain, people we have harmed, and people who have harmed us. These areas must be exposed to the light so that all darkness can be removed. You need to allow the Lord to speak to you about these things. He may have you do something, like talk an issue over with someone you harmed, or speak to your mother who abandoned you, or He may allow memories to come back just so that you can see why you went through what you went through.

MOVING FORWARD

Allow the Lord to minister to you. Don't be afraid to ask questions. God is not afraid of any of your questions. Not even "Why did I have to go through that pain?" People in church are afraid to ask God why. But God is not afraid of your why. He will show you. You may have needed to go through that experience so that after you are healed and delivered, you can help someone else who has gone through it. Wait in His presence. Listen to His voice.

One night during my process, I was before the Lord in my home. The Lord showed me different things that I had gone through as a child. Memories raced through my mind. Flashes of past experiences came to the forefront. I saw scenes of my life flashing before me. The tears flowed as I watched. It was such a powerful experience. I cried out to the Lord and asked Him to heal me from those experiences. He was there to heal—that's why He showed me those things.

Later I spoke candidly and openly with my mother about what I had gone through in her addiction. For years I had struggled with feelings of abandonment, confusion, frustration, and inner turmoil. We had a long conversation about a whole list of events. We both cried. I let my mother know beforehand that I wanted to talk about these things—not because I wanted to put a guilt trip on her—but because I knew that it was necessary. By the end of our conversation, I let my mother know that I completely forgave her for everything that went on in my life throughout her addiction.

This conversation was absolutely necessary not only for my healing but so that both of us could move on.

I had never fully shared all of these things with my mother because I hated to see her feel bad. I hated to see her cry. I did not ever want her to have guilt. If your motives are pure for bringing up past issues, the Lord is able to get in it and complete His work. But if you have a hidden agenda for bringing up past issues with someone, like you want them to feel guilty and bad for the pain they caused you, then the devil will sow his seeds of guilt, shame, unforgiveness, and depression. Time needs to be spent in the presence of the Lord so that He can purify your motives.

From that point on, I moved forward. The release brought freedom and healing. Those issues of abandonment and neglect have been cultivated, and seeds of righteousness have been planted there. Now I can be effective in sharing my experiences with other teenagers who struggle in similar areas with their parents. God had a plan. The devil had a plan but God's plan prevailed. The patriarch Joseph, years after he had been betrayed by his brothers and sold into slavery, looked back on his experiences and said, "But as for you, ye thought evil against me; but God meant it unto good, to bring to pass, as it is this day, to save such people alive" (Gen. 50:20).

SOWING IN TEARS

Although this stage of the process can be painful, I believe that it is necessary to experience true freedom. It may cost some tears, but that's all right. The psalmist wrote:

They that sow in tears, shall reap in joy. He that goeth forth and weepeth beareth precious seed, shall doubtless come again with rejoicing, bringing his sheaves with him. (Ps. 126:5–6)

Weeping may endure for a night, but joy cometh in the morning. (Ps. 30:5)

These verses comfort us when the tears flow. They are necessary. Before I got saved, I used to hate to cry—especially in front of people. But now that I am saved, weeping in the Lord's presence is beautiful to me. Sometimes I weep at the wonder of who He is. Sometimes it's because I'm so grateful for how far He has brought me. Sometimes it is out of frustration. Sometimes I cry tears of suffering. Sometimes there are tears of repentance. I have also cried tears of warfare. "When I cry unto thee, then shall mine enemies turn back: this I know; for God is for me" (Ps. 56:9). Other times I weep out of my pain which sometimes has involved pain from my past. Don't be afraid of tears. Your purging often occurs through these tears. That pain is released in His presence and replaced with joy and healing. Much pain produces much power.

In this stage of the process God delivered me from the weight of many of my past experiences and issues. Some things still need work and a bit more tilling, but I am not held in frustration or bondage to those areas. I am well aware of the issues in my life that are still in process. Some issues take more time than others. We cannot have a microwave mentality when it comes to process. I can say that many of my issues have been processed out.

I have a question for you. How far are you willing to go to be delivered? How badly do you really want it? If you take the plunge, the Lord will bring you up healed and walking in a greater level of his anointing. You can stay where you are if you want. You can slide your way into heaven and in the meantime live in bondage here on earth. But I challenge you to allow the Lord to take you through the process of deliverance. Whatever you struggle with, the Lord is able to deliver you out of that thing, and He is also able to deliver that thing out of you.

You have to be willing to take this journey with the Lord. It involves a trip down memory lane, a look back into your past.

Some restoration, renovation, and reconciliation need to occur. Some forgiveness needs to flow in your life.

> And when you stand praying, forgive, if you have aught against any; that your Father also which is in heaven may forgive you your trespasses. But if you do not forgive, neither will your Father which is in heaven forgive your trespasses.
> (Mark 11:25–26)

This is serious. Read it again and ponder what this says to you. Who is the Lord telling you to forgive? Come into His presence so that He can release you, and so that you can release them. No matter what they did to you, you have to allow the Holy Spirit to release you from the pain so that you can forgive them.

PULLED UP BY THE ROOT

The issues in your life need to be dug up by the root. If you are pulling weeds, you cannot pull out only half the weed and think that you have completed your weed-pulling activities. No. If you don't pull that weed out by the root, that weed will just grow back. We have some weeds in our lives that need to be pulled up by the root. If we don't allow the Holy Spirit to get it by the root, it won't be long before that issue arises in your life again.

The life of that thing is in the root. That thing needs to be pulled out to complete the death process. You have to allow God's hand to reach way down deep and pull that thing out of you. Allow the Word of God to be planted in that ground and fresh fruit will grow. Jesus said, "I am the true vine, and my Father is the husbandman. Every branch in me that beareth not fruit he taketh away: and every branch that beareth fruit, he purgeth it, that it may bring forth more fruit" (John 15:1–2).

One night, I had a dream. In this dream I was in a bathroom with my mother. We were looking at slides of photographs being projected onto the wall. One of those slides included a picture of the girl with whom I lived with for two years and was in the lesbian relationship. She looked very sick in the pictures.

"That's sad," my mother said in this dream as we looked at this girl's picture.

"What's sad, Mom?"

"Don't you know that she died?"

"No, I didn't know that."

I was shocked. When I woke up, the Lord gave me insight into the dream. He showed me that the issue of homosexuality is dead to me.

A few days after this dream, I shared with a Christian sister my testimony of deliverance from homosexuality. She looked at me and said, "There is no residue from that lifestyle on you." There was no longer any fruit of that lifestyle in my life. I knew at that point that the root had been cut out of me. "And now also the axe is laid unto the root of the trees; therefore every tree which bringeth not forth good fruit is hewn down, and cast into the fire" (Matt. 3:10).

MY NEED FOR LOVE

I have discovered that the thing that I wanted most in my life was love. I just wanted to feel loved. The love of a mother is what I wanted most of all, but I was willing to get it from whoever would give it to me. I searched for love in people for so many years. Once I found someone who would shower me with love and attention, I thrived off it. My world began to center around that person. This person would be a female.

I had male friends and even a couple boyfriends whom I loved, and who loved me, but it wasn't the same. I craved the love and attention from a female. As I got older, this is where the switch in my spirit happened. Love developed into sexual infatuation and lust. The root of this love was corrupt; therefore, the fruit of this love was corrupt.

I had some deep emotional wounds from my past that followed me for many years. The void for love, like a black hole, was eternally deep. Nothing could fill my void. I needed love on such a deep level. I tried to fill it with friendships and sexual relationships with men and women. I often numbed the pain with marijuana and alcohol, but these chemicals usually just intensified my feelings. I searched through an endless maze. I discovered that the love that I was searching for could only be found in Jesus Christ. I needed to be rooted and grounded in His love (See Eph. 3:17).

Once He came into my life and filled my heart with His love, everything began to change. My inward man began to be renewed day by day (See 2 Cor. 4:16). I began to feel and understand what true love was all about. The love of God can only be experienced in His presence. It emanates from His people. This was different from any love that I had ever experienced.

If you read through my journal, you would see that love is a recurring theme in my writings. You can hear the frustration in my tone when I was in the world. After salvation, my writings still carry the recurring theme of love. Now it contains a tone of satisfaction, peace, comfort, and safety, however. I have found the love for which I had been searching for years. This love healed my wounds. God's love is everlasting, unchanging, and unconditional. It's exactly what I was looking for. I found it in my Lord and Savior Jesus Christ.

There is nothing like the love of God. It reaches you in your deepest and darkest moments. It holds you through the storms of your life. The love of God is more powerful than anything I have ever known. I can actually feel the presence of the Lord and His love for me. His love will draw you closer and closer.

Do you know what is amazing? Even with all of my faults, failures, and character defects, He loves me anyway. He loves me in spite of myself. Oh, what kind of love is this! It's a love that I have never experienced before. This is the love that I searched for throughout my life. Nothing can separate me from the love of God, and nothing can compare to it.

My God, this is a love that you have to come to know for yourself. Words cannot give this love justice. You need to experience the love of God. If you have not, all you have to do is repent of your sins and ask Jesus Christ to come into your heart. He will come right in and make Himself at home. You will experience love like no other.

13. FOR A TESTIMONY

Throughout our walk in this life, we have many experiences, many trials, and many pains . . . both in the world and as a Christian. Some of the things that we go through are a result of our own disobedience. Some things may be the result of events beyond our control. We have to realize that God allows us to go through things for a purpose.

UNDERSTANDING GOD'S WAYS

Nothing that goes on in your life happens by accident. Your entire life has been strategically ordered by the Lord. Even in our disobedience, when we allow the enemy legal access to our lives, the Lord is ultimately in control. His eyes are in every place, and He is the only one who is all powerful.

I often wondered why I had to go through the things that I went through as a child. The question of why plagued my mind for many years. I can remember being in the world and wondering about God's ways. It was never hard for me to believe that God existed. But trying to understand His ways confused me. Why did I have to go through the things that I went through? I did not understand it. What was life all about? Here is an excerpt from my journal:

Why was I brought into this world? Such a selfish, non-caring, unappreciative society! What is the purpose of my existence? Is it to be a friend to the people that I care about? Is it to make something of the person that I am? Or perhaps it is to constantly give my love and never receive it from another. I don't know. But I often sit here on my bed and wonder. Is life really worth living? If so, then for what? To love or to be loved? I guess no one really knows. I sure as hell don't.

You can sense the frustration that I felt at this point in my life. I have always been a person who feels intensely. I could wear a mask on the outside and fool others about what was really going on inside me. Before my conversion, when I felt close enough to share with someone, I often expressed my feelings deeply. Sometimes I left the listener feeling awestruck about what was really going on. Even in those conversations, I never felt understood. I always felt my feelings were much deeper than words could express.

Back then I didn't realize there was a reason why I went through so much. There was a reason that my feelings were so intense. There was a purpose for my existence. Nothing in my life was happenstance. All along God had a plan for my life. He had a calling for me that would be fulfilled. This calling required that I go through some challenges for the purpose of reaching others.

God knew many teenagers would come into my life. I met many broken youth who were hungry for love. From my experience they learned that they would not find that love through relationships, sex, and drugs. Only God could show them the love they sought in others. Even though their parents abandoned them, God would never leave them nor forsake them.

God can restore their relationships with their parents. God can deliver their parents from years of drug addiction. Even though they had been molested, God can heal them. God can take away the fear of abandonment. When no one else is there, Jesus Christ wants to be there for them. He gave His life so that they could be saved.

God knew people needed to hear my testimony. Those living in the homosexual lifestyle need to know that He can deliver. They need to know that He has seen everything that they have been through—the rapes, the molestations, the abandonment, the rejection, the fear, the torment, the abuse, the neglect, and the violated trust. God sees their need to be loved by anyone who is willing to give it, even if they can feel it only through sex.

God wanted people who would be willing to share about their past so that others would be born into His kingdom. At the time, I had no idea that I would be one of the people that He would use. I mean, look at where I come from. Look at my family. Look at my lifestyle.

GOD GETS THE GLORY

Despite my seeming limitations, I had hope. Why? Because I have discovered that God often uses for His glory what society writes off as the scum of the earth.

> But God hath chosen the foolish things of the world to confound the wise; and God hath chosen the weak things of the world to confound the things that are mighty; And base things of the world which are despised, hath God chosen, yea, and things which are not, to bring to nought things that are: That no flesh should glory in his presence. (1 Cor. 1:27–29)

This is the way God operates. This is how He loves to show off. This is what He is proud of. God takes messed up lives, completely turns them around, and then uses them for His glory. By working in the lives of these people, God knows that He will get the glory. Everyone knows only God could make such a drastic transformation. God loves it.

Our problem is that we want to deny the Lord of His glory. We want everyone to see where we are in God, but we don't want to reveal all that we had to go through to get here. It amazes me how church people get amnesia after God cleans them up. They forget about where they were when the Lord reached down and got them. Now they flip up their noses at those people who are where they used to be. They act as if they are too clean to be around those who are stuck in the miry clay. This prideful attitude repulses God. He absolutely hates it.

There is a difference between a brag-a-mony and a testimony. A brag-a-mony is when a person shares past experiences because they take pride in telling others what unwholesome things they used to do. A brag-a-mony brings glory to self rather than glory to God. A testimony, on the other hand, shares past experiences to glorify the One who brought you through. When a person shares his testimony, it allows others to know that God can deliver them too.

A testimony gives glory to God. A testimony echoes the fact that if God had not rescued them from that place, they would still be there. A testimony allows people who are still struggling to see that God can turn it around for them too. A testimony brings hope to others. A testimony given under the anointing breaks shackles off the lives of people who are bound.

When Jesus met the woman at the well, He told her, "Go call your husband." She had been married five times, and the man she was with was not her husband. Looking beyond her unsavory past, Jesus spoke with her and revealed that He was the Messiah. What did this woman do?

> The women then left her waterpot, and went her way into the city, and saith to the men, Come, see a man, which told me all things that I ever did: is not this the Christ.... And many of the Samaritans of that city believed on him for the saying of the woman, which testified, He told me all that I ever did. (John 4:28–29, 39)

God wants to use you to share your testimony. He wants others to see what He can do in the life of the "scum of the earth" as well as in the life of the rich man. Don't be ashamed. Share your testimony. Show your scars to someone else so that they can see that healing can take place.

A scar is a mark that is left when a wound is healed. The scar reminds you what you went through. A scar doesn't hurt. You no longer feel the pain of the wound because it has been healed. But we do not like scars. We feel that they are ugly blemishes that detract from our beauty. But your scars are there for a purpose. Your scar testifies that healing has occurred. Your scar is a testimony that you made it through. The wound may have had the potential to kill you, but it didn't.

Your scar gives you the opportunity to share about your experience. Your scar reminds you where you came from. If you hide your scar, no one ever knows that you were once wounded and now are healed. No one ever knows that you have undergone surgery. Do not cover your scar. Expose it so that others with open, bleeding wounds can be healed and delivered.

OVERCOMING SHAME

With a testimony like mine, I understand what it means to be ashamed of your past. I understand what it feels like not to want others to know. I understand what it feels like to want to put your testimony on a shelf and forget about it. I was so ashamed.

I have testified of deliverance from homosexuality while still in bondage to shame. Sometimes I knew that I needed to testify because someone in church that day needed to hear that God can deliver from homosexuality. I testified out of obedience to the Holy Spirit, but I still had shame. How do we get the victory? "They overcame him, by the blood of the lamb, and by the word of their testimony; and they loved not their lives unto death" (Rev. 12:11).

The devil wanted me to feel ashamed. He did not want me to testify. He sure didn't want me to testify under the anointing. Even if I did testify, it didn't hold the power that it would have if I hadn't been bogged down with shame. One of the enemy's greatest tactics is to bind us with shame about where the Lord has brought us from. He knows that if we share under the anointing, others will come to know Jesus Christ as Deliverer.

Although I have come a long way in battling shame, I believe this book will bring a final deliverance for me. No more shame. I have nothing to hide anymore. My life is an open book to whoever will read this. I have nothing to be ashamed of. Jesus Christ has truly paid it all. Now it's no longer about me, but what the Lord wants to do through me. I must lose my life rather than save it. I have put my life and my struggles on paper in the hopes that someone else will become free. Now is the time.

Look at the state of the world. Look at the times we live in. Men marrying men and women marrying women. Teenagers dressing in drag. Homosexual churches. Gay bishops. Gay couples adopting children. Homosexuality being promoted on prime time television. Disneyland, "The Happiest Place on Earth," hosting one of the biggest gay events of the year annually. Gay pride marches. Gay proms.

Now is not the time to be ashamed. These people need to know that Jesus can deliver them from the bondage of homosexuality. He can set them free, just like He did for me. This is my testimony.

SOMEONE NEEDS YOUR TESTIMONY

I urge you, by the unction of the Holy Spirit, to go through your process of deliverance. Someone needs to know how far God has brought you. They need to know what had you bound. You have a testimony that someone needs to hear. Their life depends on it. Their soul depends on it. Do not allow shame to hold you captive. The more you share your testimony, the freer you become. You are a living testimony. A living epistle, "known and read of all men" (2 Cor. 3:2). You are the word that someone needs. One word from God can change a life. You are that word, if your life is hid in Christ. Let Him use you for His glory.

For we preach not ourselves, but Christ Jesus the Lord; and ourselves your servants for Jesus' sake. For God who commanded the light to shine out of darkness, hath shined in our hearts, to give the light of the knowledge of the glory of God in the face of Jesus Christ. But we have this treasure in earthen vessels, that the excellency of the power may be of God, and not of us. (2 Cor. 4:5–7)

I'm not much—just an earthen vessel. How about you? The real worth in our lives is Christ, our treasure, and what He has done for us. Let people see Christ in you, but also let them see the earthen vessel—the cracks, the dings, the chips. That makes it all the more amazing that our glorious Redeemer lives inside such flawed vessels.

14. THE GREATER GLORY

You will suffer in this life. Whether or not you are a Christian, at times you will have to suffer. It is a part of life. There is no getting around it. You will suffer some things at the hands of others. Some things you will suffer as a consequence of your own actions. Some things you suffer will be completely out of your control. Some things you suffer will be agonizing and traumatic. Some sufferings will be momentary while others will be lengthy and drawn out.

SUFFERING AS A CHRISTIAN

Rich people suffer. Poor people suffer. From the White House to the prison house, people suffer. From the big house to the crack house, people suffer. White people suffer. Black people suffer. Asians suffer. People from all different ethnicities, religious affiliations, genders, and ages all suffer. Christians too will suffer.

Beloved, think it not strange concerning the fiery trial which is to try you, as though some strange thing happened unto you: But rejoice, inasmuch as ye are partakers of Christ's sufferings; that, when his glory shall be revealed, ye may be glad also with exceeding joy. (1 Pet. 4:12–13)

In other words, don't be amazed when it is your turn to suffer, like something uncommon has happened to you. Look at Jesus. None of us, even in our very worst sufferings, suffered like He did. Because we will be glad when His glory is revealed, we are commanded to rejoice.

Throughout my life I endured suffering. When my mother was in prison, I suffered. When that man fondled me, I suffered. When I had to move in with friends because of my parents' addictions, I suffered. When I was living in the homosexual lifestyle, I suffered. I suffered some things while in the world. My suffering doesn't compare to what some people go through but, nevertheless, I suffered.

As a Christian, I have also suffered. When I answered the call that the Lord had placed on my life, the Lord separated me from my friends. This marked my first experience with suffering as a Christian. I was exceptionally close with three people. They had been there with me through some of my roughest moments. The four of us were really tight for about eight years. We had been through a whole lot together. Having these three in my life always comforted me. I had the mentality that as long as I had them, I could go on.

When I gave my life to the Lord, however, some changes began to happen inside me. I didn't want to participate in the same things anymore. I knew I had to move on. I loved the Lord more than anything or anybody, and the Lord was calling me to go with Him. I had to let go, but it hurt. It was as if the security blanket had just been torn out of the hand of a toddler. I shed many tears. I had a longing, not to do what I used to, but to be with the people whom I had grown to love so very much. Some nights I cried myself to sleep. This was suffering.

"WHY ARE YOU LOOKING BACK?"

A few years into my salvation, one of those friends got carjacked. She was not physically hurt, thank God. The night that I got the news, it hit me hard. The following couple of days, I went into a slump. I thought about my friends constantly. I stayed in bed for almost an entire day. At Bible study my pastor pointed out that a spirit of oppression had influenced me. She said to me, "The Lord says, 'Why are you looking back?'" Luke 9:62 says, "And Jesus said unto him, No man, having put his hand to the plow, and looking back, is fit for the kingdom of God."

A couple of days later, I went to Los Angeles for a shut-in, which is a three-day prayer and fasting gathering. I went for the last couple days. That first night, I went to the altar and asked to be delivered from all soul ties. Someone prayed for me. Later a woman whom I had never met came over to me and said, "The Lord says, 'Why are you looking back?'" This was the same thing the Lord had just spoken through my pastor.

When God separated me from these friends, it was a process—and it definitely caused me to suffer. I still care about them deeply and want so much to see them come to know Jesus Christ in a personal way. But what things were gain to me, those I counted loss for Christ (See Phil. 3:7). Now the Lord has intertwined my life with so many beautiful people. I found that God compensated for the many losses that I felt.

> And Jesus answered and said, Verily I say unto you, There is no man that hath left house, or brethren, or sisters, or father, or mother, or wife, or children, or lands, for my sake, and the gospel's, but he shall receive an hundredfold now in this time, houses, and brethren, and sisters, and mothers, and children, and lands, with persecutions; and in the world to come eternal life. (Mark 10:29–30)

When you want to shrink back because of the losses that may come with following Christ, hold on to this verse—and be patient. God will meet your needs for friendship and fellowship.

GLORY WILL BE REVEALED

Losing old friends for the sake of Christ is only one example of suffering as a believer. In the process of deliverance from your issues, you will suffer. In separating yourself from anything that you have grown accustomed to, you will suffer. In putting down the bottle, the crack pipe, or the cigarette, you will suffer. In the stripping process you will suffer. In remembering things that we would rather forget, for the purpose of deliverance, you will suffer. In fasting, you will suffer. If you go through the process and don't give up, you will find a glory revealed in you that will not even compare to your sufferings.

> For I reckon that the sufferings of this present time are not worthy to be compared with the glory which shall be revealed in us. (Rom. 8:18)

God gets glory when His people press through whatever they are going through. He gets glory when His people stand through the tough times. He gets glory when you allow Him to process out the issues in your life. Because He gets glory out of your life, He allows His glory to rest upon you and in you. Let's look at the Amplified Version of that same verse:

> [But what of that?] For I consider that the sufferings of this present time (this present life) are not worth being compared with the glory that is about to be revealed to us and in us and for us and conferred on us! (Rom. 8:18 AMP)

Wow! What we go through cannot even be compared to the glory that will be revealed *in* us, *to* us, *for* us, and *on* us. Just hold on, my sister; hold on, my brother. You will come out with glory. God has promised to take us "from glory to glory" (2 Cor.3:18). You will know a greater height and a deeper depth of His glory. A heavier anointing will rest upon your life.

PAYING THE PRICE

Many people see men and women of greatness and say to themselves, "I want to be like them." Yet, they have no idea what that man or woman of God had to suffer to get to that place in God.

All the people see is the glory. All they see is the anointing. They don't see the pain and the sufferings. Everybody wants the anointing of God. Everybody wants the power. But not everybody will go through what it takes to get it. They want the power but don't want the pain. They don't want to pay the price. There is a price to be paid. There is a high cost. Jesus said:

> If any man come to me, and hate not his father, and mother, and wife, and children, and brethren, and sisters, yes, and his own life also, he cannot be my disciple. And whosoever doth not bear his cross, and come after me, cannot be my disciple.For which of you intending to build a tower, sitteth not down first, and counteth the cost, whether he hath sufficient to finish it? (Luke 14:26-28)

Now Jesus was not telling us to dislike our family members. He was actually letting us know that we have to be willing to love everything and everyone less than we love Him, even our own lives, in order to be to his disciple. He was saying that there is a price to be paid to follow Him. He wants us to be aware of that and to count the cost? He wants us to weigh it out. He wants us to reason within ourselves if it is worth it. How badly do you want to be delivered? How badly do you want the glory, the anointing of God, on your life? Do you want it bad enough that you are willing to go through what it takes to get it?

If you are willing to pay the price and go through the process, I can assure you that the benefits will far outweigh the sufferings. Though the cost is high, it does not compare to the glory. It does not compare to knowing Jesus. It does not compare to knowing the delivering power of God. It does not compare to knowing the peace of God. How badly do you want it? Many want the glory but don't want to go through the process to get it.

RETURNING IN POWER

After Jesus came out of the wilderness, the Bible states, "Jesus returned in the power of the Spirit into Galilee; and there went out a fame of him through all the region round about" (Luke 4:14). Jesus went into the wilderness full of the Holy Ghost. After forty days, however, He came out *in the power of the Spirit.* When Jesus came through His process, He was ready for ministry. He was ready to cast out devils. He was ready to heal the sick. Jesus came out with power. After coming out of the wilderness, Jesus went to the synagogue and read from the Book of Isaiah:

> The Spirit of the Lord is upon me, because he hath anointed me to preach the gospel to the poor; he hath sent me to heal the broken-hearted, to preach deliverance to the captives, and recovering of sight to the blind, to set at liberty them that are bruised, to preach the acceptable year of the Lord. (Luke 4:18–19)

Jesus had been prepared and made ready to go forth. His sufferings in the wilderness prepared Him for this greater glory.

The people wondered who Christ was. They said, "Is not this Joseph's son?" (v. 22). These were the very people who saw Jesus grow up. The power of the Spirit rested upon Him so heavily that even they wondered who He had become. My friend, just allow the Lord to have His way in your life. Be willing to go through the process. Be willing to suffer for a while. If you do these things, God will raise you up in such a way that people will be shocked. People will wonder what happened to you.

People from your past will be amazed at the change that has occurred in your life. They will say, "Didn't she used to be a lesbian?" "Didn't he drink and do drugs?" "Didn't she used to be so mean?" "Is that the same person?" Whatever your past issue was, if you allow the Lord to process it, people will be amazed at the transformation. How did people react when they had heard Jesus after He returned in the power of the Spirit? "And they were astonished at his doctrine: for His word was with power" (Luke 4:32).

Things will change when His glory is revealed in you. The words you speak will hold more weight. The Word of God will be spoken under the anointing. The power of God will flow through you, and lives will be changed as a result. When you go through the process, God will dramatically change your life. You will come out with a true personal relationship with Jesus Christ.

Within months of coming out of my process of deliverance, my pastor approached me about being licensed as a minister. I was shocked and humbled to say the least. They believed that I was ready and that I had already been doing the work of one. Two years later I was ordained as an elder. Who would have ever thought it could happen? Nothing but the grace of God.

KNOWING HIM

I was never striving after the title. I was pressing after Him. I just wanted to be closer to Him. I just wanted to be more like Him. I just wanted to know Him. I just wanted to be delivered from the issues of my past. The position is just a secondary result of seeking after Him. I would be crazy now to stop seeking Him. The cry of my heart is the same now as it was then—I just want to know Him. I just want to be like Him. I just want to be closer to Him. I just want His presence.

Yea doubtless, and I count all things but loss for the excellency of the knowledge of Christ Jesus my Lord: for whom I have suffered the loss of all things, and do count them but dung, that I may win Christ, and be found in him, not having mine own righteousness, which is of the law, but that which is through the faith of Christ, the righteousness which is of God by faith: that I may know him, and the power of his resurrection, and the fellowship of his sufferings, being made conformable unto his death; If by any means I might attain unto the resurrection of the dead. Not as though I had already attained, either were already perfect: but I follow after, if that I may apprehend that for which also I am apprehended of Christ Jesus. Brethren, I count not myself to have apprehended: but this one thing I do, forgetting those things which are behind, and reaching forth unto those things which are before, I press toward the mark for the prize of the high calling of God in Christ Jesus. (Phil. 3:8–14)

We must know Him not only in the power of His resurrection but in the fellowship of His sufferings. In fact, we have to know Him in the fellowship of His sufferings *before* we can know Him in the power of His resurrection. We must be willing to suffer. Yes, it is painful. Yes, it is hard. But it is absolutely necessary for your spiritual growth. You begin to die to self in suffering. The deliverance process is a death process. We are being made conformable to His death.

The apostle Paul put it like this: "I die daily" (1 Cor. 15:31). Jesus said, "If any man will come after me, let him deny himself, and take up his cross, and follow me" (Matt. 16:24). We also have a cross to carry. Our death must also occur. We must endure suffering. But it doesn't end there. We look forward to a resurrection. When we rise, we will be delivered and walking in another realm of glory.

GOD'S PLAN

You have no idea the great plans that the Lord has for your life. The place that you are in right now is just preparation for where He is taking you. You can't see it. God has a plan—a good plan.

The Greater Glory

For I know the thoughts and plans that I have for you, says the Lord, thoughts and plans for welfare and peace and not for evil, to give you hope in your final outcome. (Jer. 29:11 AMP)

Glory, power, and anointing may seem so distant that you cannot grasp them. Whatever you do, do not give up. Your deliverance may seem to take forever. Some issues require a more lengthy process than others, but don't give up. You do not know the exact moment when God will loose you into glory. It can be anytime now. Just press and hold on. Do not let go of God's hand.

For which cause we faint not; but though our outward man perish, yet the inward man is renewed day by day. For our light affliction, which is but for a moment, worketh for us a far more exceeding and eternal weight of glory. (2 Cor. 4:16–17)

Everything that you face now just prepares you for glory. Keep that in your spirit. It will encourage you to press through when it gets rough. You are going to come out of this thing with the weight of the anointing resting upon your life. Just do not give up. Move forward. Do not allow the enemy the pleasure of seeing you turn back. Do not allow him the pleasure of seeing you defeated. He wants to laugh at you as he watches you give up in the process. Do not give him the satisfaction. Pick yourself up, dust yourself off, and keep on moving.

15. Maintaining Deliverance

Once the Lord delivers you, and you have gone through the deliverance process, you must maintain your deliverance. The Holy Ghost will help you, but you have to do some things if you plan on never revisiting the place of bondage. The apostle Paul wrote, "Stand fast therefore in the liberty wherewith Christ hath made us free, and be not entangled again with the yoke of bondage" (Gal. 5:1).

Freedom and deliverance are precious. We cannot take these graces for granted. We must maintain a standard in our lives. Your standard may be different than my standard; nevertheless there must be a standard.

NO CONFIDENCE IN THE FLESH

The rule of thumb for maintaining your deliverance is do not trust your flesh. It will deceive you. The apostle Paul knew this.

> For we are the circumcision, which worship God in the spirit, and rejoice in Christ Jesus, and have no confidence in the flesh. Though I also might have confidence in the flesh. If any other man thinketh that he hath whereof he might trust in the flesh, I more: Circumcised the eighth day, of the stock of Israel, of the tribe of Benjamin, an Hebrew of the Hebrews; as touching the law, a Pharisee; Concerning zeal, persecuting the church; touching the righteousness which is in the law, blameless. But what things were gain to me, I counted loss for Christ. (Phil. 3:3–6)

The apostle Paul challenged the Philippians to check out his resume. If anyone could put confidence in the flesh, it should have been Paul. He was the religious of the religious. He was of the upper echelon of the religious sect. He was trained in the way of the law his whole life. But even after all of that, He recognized that "in my flesh dwelleth no good thing" (Rom. 7:18). This mighty man of God knew better than to put confidence in his flesh. Why do we think we can trust our flesh?

THE WORD AND PRAYER

Whatever you were doing to get through the process, you must continue. Christians love to quote Jesus' words: "If the Son therefore shall make you free, ye shall be free indeed" (John 8:36). We tend to skip what Jesus said just before that. "If you *continue* in my word, then are ye my disciples indeed; And ye shall know the truth, and the truth shall make you free" (John 8:31–32).

You must continue in His Word. The word *"continue"* means: *stay constantly, to remain, to persevere, to be permanent, and to remain in company.* The truth of God's Word made you free, and the truth of God's Word will keep you free. We must remain in His Word. I am not just talking about reading the Bible. I am talking about continually walking out this Word in our day to day living. Studying, reading, hearing, speaking, and living this Word is essential in maintaining our deliverance.

You must also continue to pray and have intimate fellowship with your Father. During the process of my deliverance, the Lord spoke to me to open our church doors at 6:00 a.m. a couple of times a week for prayer. After I had been obedient to that for a while, He spoke to me about having prayer Monday through Friday at 6:00 a.m.

I could have argued that my pastor already opens the church daily for prayer at noon. If people really want to pray, they could come at noon. Besides, I have never been a morning person and was a little timid about making a commitment that I wasn't sure that I could keep. But as I obeyed the Lord, I found out that consistency in my prayer life would be necessary for me to maintain my deliverance.

As I pray for others daily, the Lord watches over my life. Sometimes I wanted to have someone else take over the 6:00 a.m. prayer hour for good and just have my time alone with God at home. But to this day I have not been released from that hour of prayer. I have learned so much in that sweet hour of prayer. Most of all, the Lord has used it to discipline me in how to crucify my flesh. Each morning that my alarm goes off, I have to choose to crucify my flesh. Every morning the flesh would rather turn off the alarm and go back to sleep.

But morning by morning I press past the flesh and obey the Spirit. Every morning the Lord is faithful to meet me in this sweet hour of prayer. I have learned that the more that you practice crucifying the flesh, the less likely you are to be overcome by it. Prayer was necessary for your deliverance to occur, and it will be necessary for as long as we live in this flesh. The more you do it, the more you will come to love it. There is nothing like the presence of the Lord.

FASTING AND FELLOWSHIP

Mix prayer with fasting, and you will experience great power. Fasting, another way to crucify the flesh, is a necessary practice for believers. When you deny yourself food for a period of time, you tell your body that it is not in control. You tell your body that it does not dictate your life. You crucify the flesh and its fallen nature.

People fast for many reasons. Ultimately, fasting trains you to discipline yourself in not giving in to the flesh and its desires. You deny yourself food and crucify your flesh for a specific purpose. I have experienced the power of prayer and fasting. Words cannot describe the things that I have seen happen in my life as a result of fasting. For the purpose of maintaining deliverance, fasting is great because it teaches you to crucify the flesh. Whatever you have been delivered from manifested itself in one way or another through your flesh. Therefore, we have to maintain our deliverance in that area by continuing to crucify the flesh.

If you always do whatever the flesh wants to do, you will walk in the flesh. How can you avoid doing this? The apostle Paul wrote, "This I say then, Walk in the Spirit and ye shall not fulfill the lust of the flesh" (Gal. 5:16). If you practice these things, they will cause you to walk in the Spirit. If you walk in the Spirit, you will not fulfill the lusts of your flesh.

Fellowship with the saints is also a necessary tool in maintaining your deliverance. One New Testament writer exhorted believers, "And let us consider one another to provoke unto love and to good works: Not forsaking the assembling of ourselves together, as the manner of some is; but exhorting one another: and so much the more, as you see the day approaching" (Heb. 10:24–25). This is crucial. We must stay around the people of God.

Of course, it is vital for us to stay connected to a local church. I question people who call themselves the "called and chosen" but are not connected to the Body of Christ. The Lord calls us to come together for worship as well as for fun and fellowship. Something happens in the Spirit when the saints of God come together. I see the physical manifestation of the love of God through others. It is good to have common ground with folks, to share openly and honestly with others. People will help you, if you let them.

"Iron sharpeneth iron; so a man sharpeneth the countenance of his friend" (Prov. 27:17). You are sharpened by others. You need people around you who are not afraid to tell you about yourself. You need people who are not afraid to rebuke and correct you. You need people who can pray for you when storms arise. We all need this sharpening iron in our lives.

> Two are better than one; because they have a good reward for their labor. For if they fall, the one will lift up his fellow: but

woe to him that is alone when he falleth; for he hath not another to help him up. Again, if two lie together, then they have heat: but how can one be warm alone? And if one prevail against him, two shall withstand him; and a threefold cord is not quickly broken. (Eccl. 4:9–12)

Having saints in your life is absolutely essential in maintaining your deliverance. We cannot do this thing by ourselves. Fellowship with the people of God is necessary and very beneficial.

GUARD YOUR HEART

A number of things are vital to maintain your deliverance. Depending on what you have been delivered from, you have some things that you need to keep straight. You have to guard your gates. Your gates are your eyes, your ears, and your mouth. These are all ways that things come in and out of you. What you see, what you hear, and what you say are all very powerful. Your gates need to be opened to the things of the spirit and closed to those things that may cause your flesh to rise.

What you see enters your mind. You must be aware of what you place before your eyes, whether it's television, people, magazines, or books. What you listen to is also important. We need to guard our ears from filthy language, lustful conversations, and gossip. Our mouth is also a gate. It can be used to speak words of power and life or words of destruction and death. We have to be aware of these things.

In maintaining your deliverance, you will need to keep God first. He will not settle for anything less than first. He will not share you with another. Therefore, we must continually examine our relationships with people and the things of this world. Anything or anyone that you put before Christ is your god. It is idol worship. We are to have no other gods beside Him. We must examine ourselves in this area, because we can gradually allow things and people to take God's place. Self-examinations and personal inventories are necessary in maintaining your deliverance.

We have to be watchful because we can become "at ease in Zion" after the process in an area is complete. We can become complacent and end up back in the wilderness. Now you know that the Lord is on your side. You know that you can access the presence of God any time. You know that the Lord has fought your enemies. You know that you have been brought out of bondage. You know that you have been delivered.

In all this knowing, you can forget what it took to get to this place. Egypt can seem so far removed from you that you no longer feel the need to press into the Promised Land. You can take the grace of God for granted. You will soon begin to dabble in areas that you used to avoid. You will find yourself messing around in demonic territory, using the excuse that you are delivered, so it's okay.

You can become proud and haughty. You can put God on the back burner by praying, fasting, and reading the Word only when you *feel* like it. You attend church when you *feel* like it. We have got to watch it. We have to keep a close relationship with God. Recognize that your enemy has only departed for a season. He will be back. Just because you have been delivered from an area doesn't mean that you cannot be brought back into bondage. Whether it's the same issue or a new issue, bondage is just bondage. The enemy wants you to be in bondage.

"Wherefore let him that thinketh he standeth, take heed lest he fall" (1 Cor. 10:12). This word heed comes from the Greek word *blepo*. It is a verb, an action word. In other words, it involves some constant action on your part. This word is translated to look at, behold, beware, perceive, and see. To take heed is to actively and continuously watch. The Bible tells us to take heed to ourselves (See Mark 13:9). We must actively and continuously watch ourselves. Examine yourself. Watch yourself. Watch what you look at. Watch what you read. Watch what you listen to. Watch what you say. Watch what you do. Watch who you surround yourself with. Watch, watch, watch.

STAY FILLED AND PRESS IN

You have to realize that what you have been delivered from had the ability to kill you if it was left unprocessed. Since it has been processed out, you have to guard your heart not only from re-entrance of that thing, but from any new thing that the enemy would try to bring your way. You have set yourself up as a target for the enemy. He will try to bring other issues to entangle you in, if you give him access. You have to stay full of the things of the Spirit. If you do not remain in the things of God, you could become ensnared again. Jesus said:

> When the unclean spirit is gone out of a man, he walketh through dry places, seeking rest; and findeth none. Then he saith, I will return into my house from whence I came out; and when he is come, he findeth it *empty,* swept, and garnished. Then goeth he, and taketh with himself seven other spirits more wicked then himself, and they enter in and dwell there: and the last state of that man is worse than the first. Even so shall it be also unto this wicked generation. (Matt. 11:43–45)

Isn't that something? The house may be swept and garnished. It may look like it's all together on the outside. If that house is empty on the inside, however, it has left itself open. Not only may that spirit come back, but other spirits may return with it.

You may have the nicest car in the world, but if your gas tank is empty, it isn't going anywhere. As nice as it looks on the outside, without gas it will not operate. We can be delivered and high rolling. But if we are empty on the inside, we are not going anywhere. We can't operate in the power of the Spirit. We will not have what it takes to fend off the enemy. We have to stay off empty and constantly press in to God to be full. Your deliverance was no downhill slide. Neither is maintaining it. We have to press toward the mark for the prize of the high calling of God in Christ Jesus. (Phil. 3:14)

We are constantly bombarded by the world and its wickedness. Everywhere that we turn something wants to remind us of our old ways. Day in and day out we rub shoulders with the world. We cannot believe that we can stop with deliverance and just go on without picking up any of this world's residue. We have to put off the ways and residue of the world and put on the things of God. We must remain focused and continue to press into God.

Do not become complacent in your walk with Christ. Shake yourself when you feel comfortable where you are. You should continually long for more of God. If you are satisfied where you are at and do not have a desire to be closer with Him, then you need to check yourself. It's time for personal inventory. Something must be in the way. Get that thing out of the way and continue moving in the things of God.

Praise God! I pray that these tools will be helpful in your life. Remember that your deliverance is precious. It is not something to be played with. You must have a by-any-means-necessary mentality to maintain it. Some people may not understand some of the things that you cannot involve yourself in. You may even be criticized for the stand that you take on some issues. Some may try to tell you that all that praying and fasting is not necessary anymore. But you have to do what you have to do. It is not about what others think. At the end of the day, they are not going to be there when your mind is twisted because you lowered your standard. Whatever the standard is for you, keep that standard. The Lord has given it to you for a reason. May the Lord continue to bless and keep you as you walk with Him.

CONCLUSION

We have been given the victory through Jesus Christ. The apostle Paul wrote, "But thanks be to God, which giveth us the victory through our Lord Jesus Christ. Therefore, my beloved brethren, be ye steadfast, unmovable, always abounding in the work of the Lord, forasmuch as ye know that your labor is not in vain in the Lord" (1 Cor. 15:57–58).

We can rely on Him in times of struggle and temptation. Jesus has already won the ultimate battle. If you have received Him as Lord and Savior, then your destination is heaven. I pray that this book will help you on your journey with the Lord here on earth. You do not need to be held in bondage to issues from your past. I pray that you would be willing to walk through the process of deliverance and be made free. Whatever happens from here, *do not give up!* Remember, you did nothing to initiate His love for you, and you can do nothing to stop His love for you. Just keep on pressing forward. Your change is coming. The Lord is in love with you and is preparing you to be used for the building of His kingdom. May God bless you on your journey.

If you have never received Jesus Christ as your Lord and Savior, today is the day of salvation. He can come in and change your entire life. You will experience a love, peace, and joy that you have never known. You will also have legal access to this place we call heaven. No matter what your issues are, no matter what you struggle with right now, Jesus wants to save your soul today.

Your soul is of utmost importance. The devil has fought you hard for so many years because he wants your soul. Today is the day to win the greatest battle of your life. Jesus has made it simple for you. It is as easy as ABC. A—admit that you are a sinner. B—believe in your heart that Jesus is the Son of God. C—confess that Jesus Christ is Lord and Savior.

Conclusion

If you want Jesus Christ to come into your heart and save your soul today, then pray this prayer out loud with me:

Jesus, I admit that I am a sinner and that I need to be forgiven for my sins. I believe that You are the Son of God. Jesus, I confess You as my Lord and Savior. Save me today. Fill me with Your Holy Spirit. I give You my life for the rest of my life. Thank You for saving my soul today. In Jesus' name, amen.

If you earnestly prayed that prayer, you are saved. Confess it out of your mouth right now. Say, "I am saved." Begin to read the Bible and talk to your Father so you can grow in your new faith. Ask the Lord to lead you to a church and begin to attend regularly. May God bless you both now and forever.

SOURCES

Unless otherwise indicated, all scripture quotations are taken from the authorized King James version of the Holy Bible, Ultra Thin Reference Edition copyright 1998 by Holman Bible Publishers.

Scripture quotations marked NKJV are taken from the New King James Version of the Spirit Filled Life Bible, copyright 1991 by Thomas Nelson, Inc.

Scripture quotations marked AMP are taken from the Amplified Bible, copyright 1995 by Zondervan Corporation. Mass Market Edition.

All Greek and Hebrew word definitions taken from the new Strong's Exhaustive Concordance of the Bible by James Strong, LL.DS., S.T.D., copyright 1995, 1996 by Thomas Nelson Publishers.

All English word definitions taken from Webster's New World Dictionary.